and the envelope, please

and the envelope, please

A QUIZ BOOK ABOUT THE ACADEMY AWARDS

Richard Altman

J. B. LIPPINCOTT COMPANY
Philadelphia and New York

ACKNOWLEDGMENTS

For their help in locating the photographs used in this book, I would like to thank the staff of the Margaret Herrick Library of the Academy of Motion Picture Arts and Sciences; and for their unfailingly wise advice and suggestions, special thanks to Richard DeNeut and Larry Swindell.

PN
1993.5
.U 6
A 853
1978
June 1998

The Academy of Motion Picture Arts and Sciences, whose activities include the annual Academy Awards presentation for outstanding artistic and technical achievements in motion pictures, did not participate in the publication of this book.

All photographs courtesy of the Margaret Herrick Library of the Academy of Motion Picture Arts and Sciences.

U.S. Library of Congress Cataloging in Publication Data

Altman, Richard.
  And the envelope, please.

  1. Academy awards (Moving-pictures)—Miscellanea.
I. Title.
PN1993.5.U6A853   791.43'079   77-26775
ISBN-0-397-01279-9
ISBN-0-397-01270-5 (pbk.)

For MARCY

Contents

Introduction   9

General Quiz Number One   *11*
Best Actor Quiz Number One   *13*
Best Picture   *19*
Best Actor Quiz Number Two   *23*
Best Director   *30*
Best Actor Quiz Number Three   *36*
Humphrey Bogart   *41*
Best Picture and Director Quiz Number One   *46*
Katharine Hepburn   *50*
Best Picture and Director Quiz Number Two   *52*
Best Actress Quiz Number One   *57*
1939   *63*
Best Actress Quiz Number Two   *68*
Best Song   *73*
Best Supporting Actor Quiz Number One   *76*
Spencer Tracy   *80*
Best Supporting Actor Quiz Number Two   *82*
Bette Davis   *87*
Best Supporting Actress Quiz Number One   *91*
1951   *96*
Best Supporting Actress Quiz Number Two   *101*

What's in a Name?   *107*
Two-timers   *109*
General Quiz Number Two   *115*
True or False   *120*

Answers to the Quizzes   124
List of Pictures   157

Introduction

Over the years a certain mystique has attached itself to the annual awards presented by the Academy of Motion Picture Arts and Sciences. An Academy Award has somehow become "the award of awards." When honors are given in other fields— sports, business, whatever—the award is invariably said to be "the Oscar of the such-and-such world," and that is automatically assumed by all to be *the* highest honor.

After each year's telecast of the ceremonies, there is the inevitable grumbling about who should or should not have won, as well as complaints about the length and quality of the awards' presentation itself. Yet the event continues to attract many millions of people. Obviously, then, the awards have a unique appeal.

This book is an entertainment for those who love the movies and are fascinated, for better or worse, by the Oscars. I can only hope that anyone who ambles through the following question-filled pages will have at least some of the enjoyment I have had in putting all this together.

Note

The quizzes are all self-explanatory.

Only one rule need be mentioned. For the purposes of consistency and to keep confusion to a minimum, no "honorary" or "special" awards (including those given occasionally to children for extraordinary work) should be counted as Oscars that have been won, unless the question is phrased specifically to include such awards.

GENERAL QUIZ

NUMBER ONE

1. Name the performers listed below who received Academy Awards and the films for which they won.
   a. Henry Fonda
   b. Rosalind Russell
   c. Montgomery Clift
   d. Edward G. Robinson
   e. Greta Garbo
   f. Cary Grant
   g. Charles Chaplin
   h. Fred Astaire
   i. Ginger Rogers
   j. Irene Dunne
   k. Peter O'Toole
   l. Claude Rains
   m. Barbara Stanwyck
   n. Carole Lombard
   o. Charles Boyer

2. In each of the following duos only one of those with the same surname has been awarded an Oscar. Name the winners.
   a. ANDREWS—Dana or Julie
   b. BARRYMORE—John or Lionel
   c. BRADY—Alice or Scott
   d. COBURN—Charles or James
   e. DOUGLAS—Kirk or Melvyn

f.   FERRER—Mel or José

g.   FITZGERALD—Barry or Geraldine

h.   FONDA—Jane or Peter

i.   GRIFFITH—Andy or Hugh

j.   HAYWARD—Louis or Susan

k.   HULL—Henry or Josephine

l.   HUNTER—Jeffrey or Kim

m. JACKSON—Anne or Glenda

n.   JOHNSON—Ben or Van

o.   JONES—James Earl or Shirley

p.   KELLY—Gene or Grace

q.   KENNEDY—Arthur or George

r.   MITCHELL—Cameron or Thomas

s.   O'NEAL—Ryan or Tatum

t.   REED—Donna or Oliver

u.   SCHELL—Maria or Maximilian

v.   SCOTT—George C. or Martha

w. SMITH—Sir C. Aubrey or Maggie

x.   WAYNE—David or John

y.   YOUNG—Gig or Robert

Answers on page 124.

BEST ACTOR
QUIZ NUMBER ONE

1. Only once—in 1931–32—has there been a tie vote for Best Actor. Name the winning actors and their films.

2. Only one actor has won in consecutive years. Name him and the two films for which he won.

3. James Stewart won the Oscar for Best Actor as a reporter assigned to cover a society wedding. It is generally conceded that this was a consolation prize, since he did not win for his unforgettable performance the previous year.
   a. Name the film for which he won.
   b. Name the film from the previous year.

4. In addition to the two films just described, Stewart has received three other nominations. Name the films in which he portrayed:
   a. A man who decides to kill himself, mistakenly believing that his life has been worthless.
   b. An amiable eccentric whose best friend is an invisible animal.
   c. A lawyer named Paul Biegler who defends a soldier whose wife has been raped.

5. This talented, if somewhat mannered, character actor is most famous for being unrecognizable in several Warner Brothers ambitiously overstuffed biographical epics.
   a. Name the actor.

b. Name the picture for which he won the Oscar.

c. Name the biographical film in which he stoically portrayed a famous Mexican leader.

6. The same actor also appeared in two classic crime films.
    a. Name the film in which his last two words are, "I steal."
    b. Name the other movie, a one-word title.

7. Name the three films, in addition to his winning movie, for which the actor in questions 5 and 6 was nominated for portraying the following:
    a. A prisoner condemned to death in a very early talkie.
    b. A famous French writer defending the innocent victim of a military scandal.
    c. A dedicated, aging Brooklyn doctor.

8. He won his Oscar for a gentle film in which, as one Homer Smith, he aided a group of refugee nuns.
    a. Name the actor.
    b. Name the film.
    c. Name a film in which his name appeared between Tracy and Hepburn, the only time their "one-two" billing was altered.

9. The same actor was nominated for a film about two escaped convicts who are handcuffed together.
    a. Name the film.
    b. Name his also-nominated co-star.
    c. Name the versatile actor and folk singer who received a Best Supporting Actor nomination for his role as the convicts' sympathetic pursuer in the picture.

10. He won for his electrifying performance in a courtroom, and he is unique in having had no higher than fifth billing in his winning film.
    a. Name the actor.
    b. Name the film.
    c. Name at least two of the four performers billed above him.

11. Before Peter Sellers took over, he was the actor most frequently associated with England's best comedies. However, he won his

Oscar for his portrayal of an obsessive British officer, Colonel Nicholson, in a prisoner-of-war drama.

    a.   Name the actor.

    b.   Name the movie.

    c.   Name the American actor who co-starred with him.

    d.   Name the Japanese actor who played Colonel Saito.

12. One of Britain's most accomplished actors, he seldom ventures into films. He scored re-creating his stage triumph as a famous figure in English history.

    a.   Name the actor.

    b.   Name the movie.

    c.   Name the actresses who played the wife and daughter.

13. He earned his greatest fame as a supremely stupid sewer worker named Ed Norton on television. His winning performance on the big screen was his portrayal of an old man who travels with his beloved cat.

    a.   Name the actor.

    b.   Name the film.

    c.   Name a film in which, co-starring with Lily Tomlin, he played an over-the-hill private detective.

14. Although this German actor won the first Best Actor award for both *The Way of All Flesh* and *The Last Command*, he is better remembered by most people today for his role as a professor who falls hopelessly in love with a singer in a sleazy nightclub.
    a. Name the actor.
    b. Name the film in which he was the smitten professor.
    c. Name the actress who played the coldhearted singer.

15. Another early winner, although he won his Oscar playing the Cisco Kid in the film, *In Old Arizona*, is also more famous for another role: a Broadway director who pushes a nervous understudy onstage, assuring her that she will be "coming back a star!"
    a. Name the actor.
    b. Name the musical in which he played the director.
    c. Name the actress who played the understudy and who has always been associated with that particular role.
    d. Name the Columbia series of B movies in which this actor later starred in the title role.

16. This stalwart actor is closely associated with biblical epics and, more recently, "disaster" movies. His award was for playing the title role in MGM's multimillion-dollar remake of one of its silent classics.
    a. Name the actor.
    b. Name the film.
    c. In what film did he portray Moses?
    d. Name a popular film in which he played an astronaut who came upon a strange civilization.

17. A member of a famous theatrical family, he won his Oscar playing an iconoclastic lawyer in a film in which Norma Shearer and Clark Gable also appeared.

    a. Name the actor.

    b. Name the picture.

    c. Name the character he portrayed in MGM's B-movie hospital series, in which he appeared with Lew Ayres.

    d. Name the only film in which he appeared with both his brother and sister.

18. The same actor, whose voice has always been a favorite of mimics, played many memorable roles at MGM and elsewhere.

    a. In which Frank Capra film did he play the nontaxpaying, grandfatherly head of a highly unorthodox family?

    b. In which other Capra film did he portray the richest, meanest man in town?

    c. What is the MGM film in which he and wife Billie Burke were to host an all-star gathering?

19. One of the most debonair and durable of leading men won his award as a bogus major who is caught up in a tawdry scandal at a proper little English hotel.

    a. Name the actor.

    b. Name the film.

    c. Name the actress who played the timid girl he befriended.

20. This often dynamic actor won his Oscar playing a Southern sheriff who is forced to work alongside a black detective to solve a crime.

    a. Name the actor.

    b. Name the movie.

    c. What is the title of another of this actor's films, in which he memorably portrayed an elderly survivor of a Nazi concentration camp?

Answers on page 124.

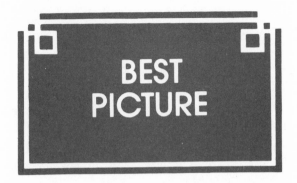

BEST PICTURE

The films in this quiz won the Academy Award for Best Picture, although the directors did not win Oscars for their work on these films.

1. The first Academy Award for Best Picture went to a film about the early days of aviation. It featured Richard Arlen, Clara Bow, Charles "Buddy" Rogers, and Gary Cooper. Name the picture.

2. This film of the seventies was made in two parts. Each won the Best Picture Oscar in its year of release. Name the title of the film that did *not* also win the Best Director award.

3. The title of this Warner Brothers "biography" suggested that it would be another in that studio's series of opulent historical productions, this one concerning a famous French writer. It concentrated primarily, however, on that celebrity's involvement with the notorious Dreyfus case. Name the film.

4. The director of the preceding film was:
   a. Michael Curtiz
   b. William Dieterle
   c. Anatole Litvak

5. The first musical to win the Best Picture award was produced, appropriately enough, by MGM. The studio incorporated the same title in three later musicals made in 1936, 1938, and 1940. Name the winning film.

6. In an extremely colorful and popular movie about circus life, Betty Hutton was top-billed in what was to be her last major appearance, Charlton Heston co-starred in the first of his many king-sized productions, and James Stewart was mysteriously disguised as a clown. Name the film.

7. Name the director of the preceding film, who never received a Best Director award.

8. Every all-star, multi-plotted movie owes a debt to this timeless MGM film, based on a Vicki Baum novel with a German locale.
    a. Name the picture.
    b. Name at least four of the stars.
    c. Name the remake, which starred Ginger Rogers, Walter Pidgeon, Van Johnson, and Lana Turner.

9. Several of Shakespeare's plays have been filmed and have met with varying degrees of success.
    a. Name the only one of these films to win the Best Picture Oscar.
    b. Name the director of this film.
    c. Name two other Shakespearean films directed by this same person.

10. *A Midsummer Night's Dream, Julius Caesar,* and *Romeo and Juliet* are among other plays by Shakespeare that have reached the screen.
    a. Name at least three of the stars of Warners' *A Midsummer Night's Dream.*
    b. Name at least three of the stars of MGM's *Julius Caesar.*
    c. Name at least two of the couples who played the "star-cross'd lovers" in English-language films of *Romeo and Juliet.*

11. A taut thriller about a black detective who skillfully works along-side a redneck Southern sheriff was a surprise winner over *Bonnie and Clyde* and *The Graduate.* Name the film.

12. An ambitious ballet, danced and choreographed by Gene Kelly, was the concluding highlight of this entertaining musical with a rather thin story and a strong Gershwin score.
    a. Name the film.

b. Name the French dancer-actress who made her American debut in this movie.

c. Name the producer and director, both associated with many of MGM's best musicals.

13. Mr. Christian and Captain Bligh are the central characters in this sea saga.

a. Name the film.

b. Name the two actors who played Christian and Bligh in the original production.

c. Name the two actors who played those roles in MGM's unfortunate and costly remake.

14. The only Western to win was a very early sound film starring Irene Dunne and Richard Dix as Sabra and Yancey Cravat. Name the movie.

15. A timid young bride, the second wife of the brooding owner of a huge English estate, is confronted with an ominous, menacing atmosphere and a strangely sinister, jealous housekeeper. Adapted from a Daphne du Maurier novel, this was David O. Selznick's first production to follow *Gone With the Wind*.

a. Name the film.

b. Name the director who made his American debut with this film.

c. Name the performer who played the title role.

16. The director of the preceding film made two others for Selznick, both of which starred Gregory Peck.
  a. Name the film in which Peck was mentally disturbed and for which Salvador Dali contributed to the dream sequences.
  b. Name the film in which Peck played an English barrister and Louis Jourdan and Valli (later known as Alida Valli) made their American debuts.

17. A scorching film adaptation of a Robert Penn Warren novel, this was the story of an ambitious politician named Willie Stark who achieved the power that was to corrupt him. Name the film.

18. The film just described was written for the screen and directed by:
  a. Edward Dmytryk
  b. Mark Robson
  c. Robert Rossen

19. A long, expensive MGM tribute to a great Broadway producer, this winning film featured *The Thin Man* co-stars in the leading roles and a Viennese actress who won an Oscar for her brief appearance.
  a. Name the film.
  b. Name the leading actor and actress.
  c. Name the characters these two performers played.

20. Another great showman, Mike Todd, made only one film, but it was truly spectacular. Adapted from a Jules Verne story, it was the tale of a supercilious Englishman named Phileas Fogg and his heroic efforts to win an ambitious bet.
  a. Name the movie.
  b. Name the actor who played Fogg.
  c. Name the actor who played Fogg's servant, Passepartout.

Answers on page 126.

BEST ACTOR
QUIZ NUMBER TWO

1. His stage reputation gave this actor and his films an aura of class. He won his third Best Actor award in the title role of a film about a British prime minister.
    a. Name the actor.
    b. Name the film.
    c. Name the actress he was responsible for casting in *The Man Who Played God*, her first film for Warners.

2. His winning role was a tough, New York City detective out to trap the men who were smuggling heroin into the United States.
    a. Name the actor.
    b. Name the picture.
    c. Name the movie for which he received a Best Supporting Actor nomination for playing a bank robber named Buck Barrow.

3. MGM temporarily banished this rising young actor to a "poverty row" studio, Columbia, as punishment for being difficult. The film he made, in which he played a reporter who falls in love with an on-the-lam socialite, won multiple Oscars, including one for him.
    a. Name the actor.
    b. Name the movie.
    c. Name the brilliant comedienne to whom he was later married offscreen.

4. Always entertaining even at his hammiest, this versatile character actor gave such a robust and juicy portrayal of an English king that it has since been difficult to accept anyone else in the role.
   a. Name the actor.
   b. Name the film.
   c. Name the delightful actress to whom he was married and who appeared with him in this and other films.

5. Name the films in which this same character actor portrayed:
   a. The tyrannical father of Norma Shearer in the first film version of a play about two famous poets.
   b. A wily barrister who is nonetheless outfoxed in a superior Agatha Christie courtroom thriller.
   c. A French police officer in relentless pursuit of Fredric March.
   d. A rumpled, crafty Southern senator in a slick Otto Preminger film about behind-the-scenes maneuvering in Washington.

6. Playing a priest in his usual easygoing manner—in a genial, unpretentious, and very popular film—won the Academy Award for this actor-singer.
   a. Name the actor.
   b. Name the picture.
   c. Name the later film he was nominated for in his most ambitious performance as an alcoholic actor attempting a comeback.

7. The same actor-singer teamed up most happily with two other Paramount stars for a series of comedies that took the trio to many exotic parts of the world.

    a. Name the two other performers.

    b. Name at least three of the places they visited in this series.

8. Re-creating his Broadway success as the title character in an unashamedly romantic classic by Rostand, this actor won for his bravura performance.

    a. Name the actor.

    b. Name the film.

    c. Name the movie he later starred in, most famous for its color photography and its spirited cancan sequence, in which he played a famous French painter.

9. Generally acknowledged to be a pleasant leading man and light comedian, he surprised almost everyone with his gripping performance as an alcoholic in a harrowing Paramount film.

    a. Name the actor.

    b. Name the picture.

    c. Earlier, he co-starred with Gary Cooper and Robert Preston in the best-remembered film version of a famous adventure story. Name the film.

10. This actor hardly seemed headed for superstardom until he played a penniless screenwriter who latches onto a demented ex-star in a trenchant Billy Wilder movie. He later starred in a comedy-drama for Wilder as a rather unsympathetic con man in a Nazi prisoner-of-war camp.

    a. Name the actor.

    b. Name the film about Hollywood.

    c. Name the film about war prisoners.

    d. Nominated for both, for which film did he win?

11. Name the films in which this same actor portrayed:

    a. George Gibbs, a young man in Grover's Corners, in the film version of Thornton Wilder's play.

    b. An attractive drifter who falls in love with the town's prettiest girl, in the film version of a play by William Inge.

    c. A television news executive in an original screenplay by Paddy Chayefsky.

d. A Broadway director in a film adapted from a play by Clifford Odets.

12. This actor co-starred with Shirley Booth and Anna Magnani in their Oscar-winning films. He won his own award for a film in which he played a hypocritical minister.
a. Name the actor.
b. Name the movie.

13. Name the films in which the actor just described portrayed:
a. An Army sergeant stationed in Hawaii in 1941.
b. A German officer on trial for his life.
c. A general plotting to overthrow the United States government.
d. A convict whose hobby was caring for birds.

14. After a meteoric rise to superstardom during the war years, he finally won an Academy Award as a gentle Southern lawyer and father named Atticus Finch. Name the actor and the film.

15. Name the films for which the same actor was nominated for portraying:
   a. A young priest (his first major film).
   b. A farmer whose son's pet is a young deer.
   c. A reporter who pretends to be Jewish.
   d. A stern air force general.

16. Name the films in which the actor in questions 14 and 15 played the following:
   a. A newsman who falls in love with a princess.
   b. An obsessed, peg-legged captain of a whaling ship.
   c. A rich, hell-raising wastrel in what must be the gaudiest Western ever made.
   d. A submarine commander in Australia as civilization is about to end after a nuclear war.

17. Already established as a dependable character actor, he won his award for playing two roles in a Western spoof that co-starred him with Jane Fonda in the title role.
   a. Name the actor.
   b. Name the movie.
   c. Name the expensive musical flop he later co-starred in with Clint Eastwood and Jean Seberg.

18. In his Oscar-winning performance, he was a character who has himself committed to a mental institution. Name the actor and the film.

19. Name the films for which this same actor was nominated in the following roles:
   a. A young man trying to "find himself" after having fled from his respectable family.
   b. A veteran sailor escorting an unworldly younger man to prison.
   c. A 1930s Los Angeles private eye who, while investigating political corruption, gets his nose slashed.

20. Name the landmark counterculture film in which hippies and motorcycles were prominent and for which the actor in questions 18 and 19 received his first nomination (for Best Supporting Actor).

Answers on page 127.

BEST DIRECTOR

This quiz covers directors who won the Best Director award for films that were not named Best Picture.

1. Name the recipient of the first Best Director award—for *Seventh Heaven* in 1927–28—who won again in 1931–32 for *Bad Girl*.

2. Name the director who won the second annual award for *The Divine Lady* and later won for a movie that also captured the Best Picture Oscar. (See Best Picture and Director Quiz Number Two.)

3. The award for 1930–31 went to a director who was to have an unusually long-lasting career in Hollywood, generally making rather lightweight films. The title character in his winning film was played by the youngest person to be nominated as Best Actor, Jackie Cooper.
   a. Name the director.
   b. Name the picture.

4. Famed as a director of Westerns, none of the films for which this man was honored was in that genre. Three of his directing awards were for films that were equal or superior to those named as Best Picture.
   a. Name the director.

b. Name his thirties film which starred Victor McLaglen.

c. Name his forties film which starred Henry Fonda.

d. Name his fifties film which starred John Wayne.

5. Another multiple-award winner received one of his Oscars for a film that did not win the big prize, but it did add the word "pixilated" to our vocabulary. It was a comedy about a small-town boy who inherits a fortune, goes to New York, and—as was the custom in this director's films—ultimately triumphs over the city slickers.

a. Name the director.

b. Name the movie.

c. Name the leading actress.

6. As Lucy and Jerry Warriner, Irene Dunne and the fast-rising Cary Grant co-starred in this director's delightful "screwball" comedy about a wealthy couple who decided to divorce. The naïve dunce who unsuccessfully wooed Dunne was played, of course, by Ralph Bellamy.

a. Name the director.

b. Name the film.

7. Name the dramatic film, featuring Victor Moore and Beulah Bondi, made by this same director in the year he made his winning comedy, which many consider Hollywood's finest picture about old age.

8. For what was undoubtedly the best American film of its year—a memorable tale of gold and greed set in Mexico—screenplay and directing awards were won by the same person.

a. Name the director.

b. Name the film.

9. Another film by this director, released in the same year as the foregoing film, was an adaptation of a Maxwell Anderson play.
   a. Name the movie.
   b. Name the actor who starred in both of the director's films that year.
   c. Name the actress who won a Best Supporting Actress Oscar as a racketeer's alcoholic mistress in this film.

10. Addie Ross sends a note to three women, informing them that she has run off with one of their husbands. Thus begins a literate and absorbing comedy that investigates the lives and marriages of these women. The director of this film, who also wrote the screenplay, won Academy Awards in both categories.
    a. Name the writer-director.
    b. Name the picture.
    c. Name the actresses who played the three women.

11. Name the films described, all of which were the work of the director just described.
    a. The story of a beautiful movie star named Maria Vargas, recalled in flashback at her funeral.
    b. A Shakespearean tragedy, in which both Greer Garson and Deborah Kerr appeared.
    c. The screen version of a top Broadway musical with a grand score by Frank Loesser.
    d. An adaptation of a Tennessee Williams play in which the rich Mrs. Venable wants a lobotomy performed on young Catherine Holly.
    e. One of the most overpublicized epics ever filmed.

12. This director-choreographer created one of the most evocative and dazzling of all motion picture musicals with his version of Christopher Isherwood's Berlin stories, previously turned into a play and then a musical on Broadway.
    a. Name the director.
    b. Name the musical.

13. Earlier, the same person directed a flashy but less successful musical in which Shirley MacLaine played a kooky, warm-hearted dance-hall hostess.
    a. Name the film.

b. Name the performer who played the MacLaine role on Broadway and coached her for the film.

c. Name the Oscar-winning Italian movie on which this musical was based.

14. Another film made by this same director dealt with the self-destruction of a controversial nightclub comedian.

  a. Name the film.

  b. Name the actor, nominated for his performance, who played the title role.

  c. Name the actress, nominated for her performance, who played the comedian's wife.

15. The first of this director's two Academy Awards was for his expertly moving production of a Theodore Dreiser novel, the story of an ambitious young man who finds himself deeply in love with a rich and beautiful girl and unable to break away from a drab and pregnant factory worker.

  a. Name the director.

  b. Name the film.

  c. Name the actors who played the three principals.

16. The second of this same director's Oscars was won for a film about oil, money, and power in Texas, adapted from a sprawling Edna Ferber novel.

  a. Name the film.

  b. Name the actor who played the hero, Bick Benedict.

  c. Name the actress who played Leslie Lynnton, the girl Bick married.

  d. Name the actor who played the wildly unmanageable Jett Rink.

17. This same director made one of the finest of all Western movies, the story of an enigmatic stranger who comes to the aid of a family trying to settle in hostile territory and who is idolized by the family's little boy.
  a. Name the film.
  b. Name the actor who played the title role.
  c. Name the performers who played the husband and wife.
  d. Name the young actor who played the boy and received a Best Supporting Actor nomination.

18. Name the films described, all made by the director in the preceding three questions.
  a. The first film that teamed Tracy and Hepburn.
  b. Hepburn in the title role as a middle-class girl with social pretensions and an eye on Fred MacMurray.
  c. Via John van Druten's play, a young woman reminiscing about her family in San Francisco—especially her Norwegian-born mother, played by Irene Dunne.
  d. A group of Jews hiding from the Nazis in Amsterdam.

19. This film hit the emotional bull's-eye of the American psyche of the sixties so effectively that it became one of the most popular of all films. Its director scored for his witty and perceptive direction of the story about a young man who has an affair with an older woman and then falls in love with her daughter.
  a. Name the director.
  b. Name the movie.
  c. Name the performers who played the three principal roles.

20. Name these movies that were also made by the director just described:
  a. A black comedy with a military setting and Alan Arkin heading an all-star cast.
  b. His challenging first film, a faithful rendering of Edward Albee's most famous play.
  c. A study of sexual mores, with Jack Nicholson, Art Garfunkel, Candice Bergen, and Ann-Margret.

Answers on page 129.

13. As a mentally retarded young man who undergoes experiments to improve his condition, this actor gave his best screen performance, re-creating a role he had played earlier on television.
   a. Name the actor.
   b. Name the film.
   c. Name the British actress who co-starred with him.

14. Widely regarded as the finest actor of our time, this honored Englishman made several Shakespearean films and won a Best Actor Oscar for one of them.
   a. Name the actor.
   b. Name the film.
   c. Name at least two other Shakespearean films in which he played the title role and won a Best Actor nomination.

15. Name the films in which this same English actor has starred that were adapted from famous novels by:
   a. Emily Brontë
   b. Daphne du Maurier
   c. Jane Austen
   d. Theodore Dreiser

16. As a television news anchorman going through a mental breakdown, his award-winning performance was stunning.
   a. Name the actor.
   b. Name the film.
   c. Name an earlier film for which he was nominated, in which he portrayed a homosexual who shared the affections of a young man with Glenda Jackson.

39

17. Whether he was playing a killer, cop, coward, or hero, this actor's popularity has never diminished. In his winning performance he played the unkempt, boozy operator of a dilapidated little riverboat whose life was changed by a spinster missionary.
    a. Name the actor.
    b. Name the film.
    c. Name the portly British actor who played the spinster's brother.

18. This beefy actor reached the pinnacle of his career in a John Ford film with his performance as Gypo Nolan, a simpleminded Irishman during "the troubles," who—for a reward—was responsible for the capture of his friend (Wallace Ford).
    a. Name the actor.
    b. Name the film.
    c. Name a later Ford film in which he played Maureen O'Hara's brother and had a lengthy, spectacular fight with John Wayne.

19. Paddy Chayefsky's paean to the little people, the story of a homely Bronx butcher and the plain girl with whom he falls in love, was an early television triumph before becoming an award-winning film. This actor won his award playing the title role in the movie version.
    a. Name the actor.
    b. Name the movie.
    c. Name the earlier picture in which he played a sadistic sergeant, Fatso Judson.

20. Most of Rodgers and Hammerstein's musicals have been transferred to the screen. One of the more successful was this 1956 film in which the leading man won an Oscar re-creating his Broadway role of a proud, stubborn monarch.
    a. Name the actor.
    b. Name the film.
    c. Name another movie in which he appeared for Twentieth Century-Fox the same year, co-starring with Ingrid Bergman and Helen Hayes.

Answers on page 130.

HUMPHREY BOGART

1. Two 1941 films catapulted Humphrey Bogart to major stardom. One was a private-eye film. The other, in which he co-starred with Ida Lupino, presented him as one of his most memorable criminals, Roy Earle. Name the two films.

2. The next year he made another movie that featured him with two of the principals from the same private-eye movie, but it was in no way a sequel.
   a. Name the movie.
   b. Name the two actors with whom he was reunited.

3. A neurotic navy captain whose officers rebelled against him was one of his most famous characters and brought him his third Best Actor nomination.
   a. Name the film.
   b. Name at least two of his three co-stars.

4. Another nominated performance found him as Rick Blaine, who had been in love with Ilsa Lund, who now reappeared with husband Victor Laszlo, who was harassed by Major Strasser, who was murdered in front of Captain Louis Renault, who kept the identity of the murderer to himself. Name this immortal melodrama.

5. He was a French flier who had escaped earlier from Devil's Island and whose wife was Michele Morgan. Rains, Greenstreet,

and Lorre were all on board for this one, which is famous (or infamous) for its flashbacks within flashbacks. Name the film.

6. Name the movie in which Lauren Bacall made her screen debut opposite him in a film that took its title and part of its plot from an Ernest Hemingway story.

7. Name another film with Bacall in which, as a private eye, he got involved in an incredibly complicated plot involving Bacall's drug-addicted sister, Martha Vickers.

8. In another film with Bacall he underwent plastic surgery, and Agnes Moorehead climaxed a memorable portrayal by jumping out of a window. Name this film.

9. Name yet another film with Bacall that pitted hero Bogart against villain Edward G. Robinson. Lionel Barrymore and Claire Trevor co-starred in this film version of a Maxwell Anderson play.

10. Searching for gold, he became increasingly greedy, suspicious, and paranoid. Name this classic film.

11. Name the goofy, satirical film in which he was married to Gina Lollobrigida and a blond Jennifer Jones played a compulsive liar named Gwendolyn Chelm.

12. Name an early film in which, as an escaped convict, he kept Bette Davis, Leslie Howard, and others trapped in a roadside café.

43

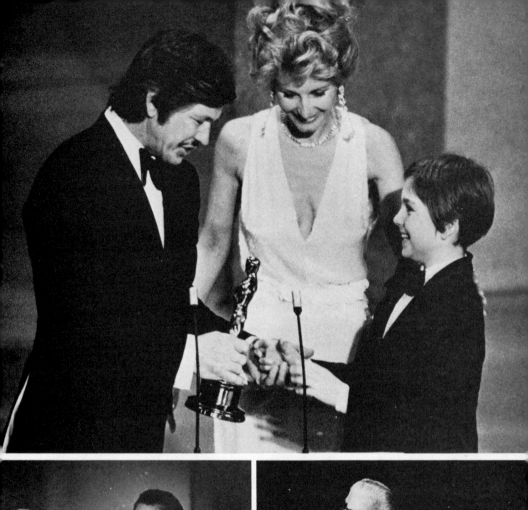

13. Name a later film in which, as an escaped convict, he held Fredric March, Martha Scott, and others as hostages in their own home.

14. Name the comedy in which he, Peter Ustinov, and Aldo Ray played escaped convicts.

15. He won his Oscar for a film directed by John Huston.
    a.   Name the film.
    b.   Name at least three of the five additional films he made under Huston's direction, all of which have been described already.

16. A most unusual Bogart played a wealthy New York businessman who won out over brother William Holden for Audrey Hepburn's affections. Name this film.

17. In Samuel Goldwyn's film version of a play that accented the proximity between Manhattan's poor and its prosperous, he played another criminal, while Sylvia Sidney starred in her usual thirties role as the poor but plucky heroine.
    a.   Name the film.
    b.   Name the gravel-voiced actress who played his mother.
    c.   Name at least two of the young toughs with whom he first appeared in this film.

18. Name the film in which, in a supporting role and sporting a less than convincing Irish brogue, he was in charge of wealthy Bette Davis's horses.

19. Barbara Stanwyck and Alexis Smith played opposite him in two thrillers which were among the last films he made under his long Warner Brothers contract. Name at least one of these films.

20. Name the films in which he portrayed:
    a.   Sam Spade
    b.   Duke Mantee
    c.   Philip Marlowe
    d.   Captain Queeg
    e.   Fred C. Dobbs
    f.   Charlie Allnut

Answers on page 131.

BEST PICTURE AND DIRECTOR
QUIZ NUMBER ONE

The Academy, sensibly enough, has most often bestowed Oscars on the film as well as its director. This quiz covers that more usual situation.

1. Only one director has won four Best Director awards, and only one film for which he was honored also won the Best Picture Oscar. It was a drama about a Welsh coal-mining village.
   a. Name the director.
   b. Name the film.

2. A major television success, this Paddy Chayefsky story of a fat, lonely butcher won many additional honors when it was made into a movie.
   a. Name the film.
   b. Name the actor, a later Oscar winner, who created the title role on television but did not play the part in the movie.

3. The film just described won the Best Director award for:
   a. Anthony Mann
   b. Daniel Mann
   c. Delbert Mann

4. One of the screen's great comedies dealt with the sometimes treacherous world of the Broadway theater.
   a. Name the movie.

b. Name at least three of the five performers who were nominated for this film.

c. Name the blonde who played an aspiring actress whose name was Miss Caswell.

5. The man who directed and wrote the brilliant screenplay for the preceding film repeated a previous coup by walking off with two Oscars for his efforts. Name him.

6. Only two films have won Academy Awards for Best Picture, Best Director, Best Actor, and Best Actress.
   a. Name the two films.
   b. Name the two winning directors.

7. The director of the first of these two multiple winners directed another film which was honored as Best Picture and for which he won his third Best Director award. The movie was an adaptation of a Kaufman and Hart play about a household filled with odd but happy nonconformists.
   a. Name the film.
   b. Name the gifted comedienne who played Alice Sycamore, the sanest member of this group.
   c. Name the actor who played Tony Kirby, Miss Sycamore's romantic interest.

8. Longfellow Deeds, Jefferson Smith, and John Doe are all leading characters in films made by the foregoing director.
   a. Name the three films.
   b. Name the actors who played the three characters.
   c. Name a later comedy-drama by this director in which the actor who was Jefferson Smith played a man about to take his own life.

9. During the forties when Darryl F. Zanuck was responsible for the high quality of Twentieth Century-Fox's output, one of the studio's strongest films dealt with anti-Semitism. Adapted by Moss Hart from a novel by Laura Z. Hobson, it focused on a Gentile writer who pretends to be Jewish.
   a. Name the film.
   b. Name the director.
   c. Name the leading actor and actress.
   d. Name the actor who played the writer's young son.

10. The director who won his first Oscar for the preceding film won his second for his direction of a Budd Schulberg story which was ostensibly about mobsters who controlled the lives of dock workers, but also dealt with the then-touchy subject of informing. Name the film.

11. This same director is justly revered for his ability to get the best possible performances from his actors, and no less than nine performers have won Oscars under his direction.
    a.   Name his film which won three acting awards.
    b.   Name his three films in which Marlon Brando starred.
    c.   Name at least two of the other five Oscar-winning actors in his films.

12. A film about an obscure boxer who gets an unexpected chance to win the title became a highly successful, award-winning movie.
    a.   Name the film.
    b.   Name the director.
    c.   Name an earlier movie made by this director for which Jack Lemmon won an Oscar.

13. Often erroneously referred to as "a woman's director," he won his award for directing a landmark American musical.
    a.   Name the director.
    b.   Name the film.

14. Name the actors, directed by the man just described, who won Academy Awards for the following performances:
    a.   A wife whose husband almost succeeds in driving her mad.

b. An actor who begins to live his roles offstage.

c. A birdbrained ex-chorus girl being kept by a rich brute named Harry Brock.

d. A magazine writer assigned to cover a socialite's wedding.

e. An expert on phonetics.

15. Two of the three films for which this distinguished director was honored dealt with people whose lives were dramatically altered by World War II. The first concerned a British family during the war; the second focused on the problems confronting veterans returning home after the war.

a. Name the director.

b. Name the two films.

16. Name the film for which the director mentioned in question 15 won his third award, the huge MGM remake of its silent biblical spectacular.

17. Only two directors have won Best Director Oscars in consecutive years. Name the directors and the films for which they each won their two awards.

18. Another early winner (for 1929–30) received the award for his great antiwar film. He also was awarded a unique "Direction–Comedy" Oscar for *Two Arabian Knights* at the first ceremony, making that first award a quasi-tie vote.

a. Name the director.

b. Name the antiwar film.

c. Name the film's leading man.

19. Only once have there been two Best Director awards for the same picture. One of the winners also received a special award for the film's brilliant choreography.

a. Name the director who won two awards.

b. Name the other director.

c. Name the movie.

20. The "other director" described in question 19 won a second Academy Award for a syrupy but tremendously popular Rodgers and Hammerstein musical. Name the picture.

Answers on page 132.

KATHARINE HEPBURN

Name the films in which Katharine Hepburn portrayed:

1. An intellectual newswoman named Tess Harding opposite a down-to-earth sportswriter played by Spencer Tracy in their first film together.

2. A spirited young woman who, alongside a spectacled Cary Grant, searched for a leopard and a bone in one of the best of the "screwball" comedies.

3. The younger sister of a debutante engaged to a carefree young man, again played by Cary Grant, who discovers he has more in common with Hepburn than with his fiancée.

4. The tomboyish heroine in a film based on a famous sentimental novel, in which she had three loving sisters.

5. The drug-addicted mother of a tubercular son in the screen version of a great American play.

6. A lawyer defending a featherbrained murderess, who is being prosecuted by Hepburn's husband, played by Tracy.

7. A farmer's daughter whose life is enriched by an itinerant con man, Burt Lancaster.

8. A missionary named Rose Sayer who flees from the Germans on a small riverboat with a man named Charlie Allnut.

Nobody would ever believe that I would travel 350 miles every weekend just to be with one girl.

(Especially if they knew it was back roads almost the whole way.)

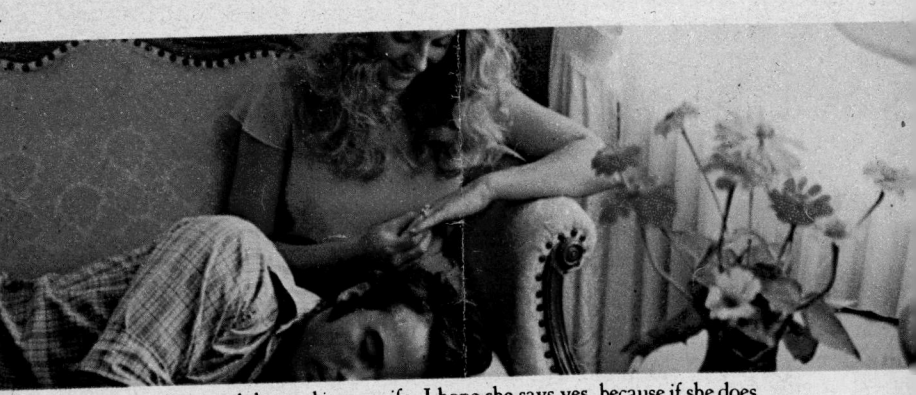

Today I'm going to ask her to be my wife. I hope she says yes, because if she does, well, think what I'll save on gas.

A diamond is forever.

1. **Katharine Hepburn**, with three Best Actress Oscars (for "Morning Glory," "Guess Who's Coming to Dinner" and "The Lion in Winter").

2. **Walter Brennan**, with three Best Supporting Actor Oscars (for "Come and Get It," "Kentucky" and "The Westerner").

3. **John Ford**, with four Best Director Oscars (for "The Informer," "The Grapes of Wrath," "How Green Was My Valley" and "The Quiet Man"). In addition, Ford directed two Oscar-winning Best Documentary Short Subjects, "The Battle of Midway" and "December 7th."

4. **"Ben-Hur,"** with 11 Oscars: including Best Picture, Best Actor (Charlton Heston), Best Supporting Actor (Hugh Griffith), Best Director (William Wyler), Best Musical Score (Miklos Rozsa), and Best Cinematography (Robert L. Surtees). Counting honorary Oscars, "West Side Story" matches this record.

5. **Katharine Hepburn**, with 11 Best Actress nominations (for "Morning Glory," "Alice Adams," "The Philadelphia Story," "Woman of the Year," "The African Queen," "Summertime," "Suddenly, Last Summer," "Long Day's Journey into Night," "Guess Who's Coming to Dinner," and "The Lion in Winter").

6. **Spencer Tracy**, with nine Best Actor nominations (for "San Francisco," "Captains Courageous," "Boys Town," "Father of the Bride," "Bad Day at Black Rock," "The Old Man and the Sea," "Inherit the Wind," "Judgment at Nuremberg" and, posthumously, "Guess Who's Coming to Dinner").

7. **William Wyler**, with 12 Best Director nominations (for "Dodsworth," "Wuthering Heights," "The Letter," "The Little Foxes," "Mrs. Miniver," "The Best Years of Our Lives," "The Heiress," "Detective Story," "Roman Holiday," "Friendly Persuasion," "Ben-Hur" and "The Collector").

8. **"All About Eve,"** with 14 nominations including: Best Picture, Best Actress (Anne Baxter), Best Actress (Bette Davis), Best Supporting Actress (Celeste Holm), Best Supporting Actor (George Sanders), Best Supporting Actress (Thelma Ritter), Best Director (Joseph L. Mankiewicz), Best Screenplay (Mankiewicz), Best Musical Score (Alfred Newman).

9. **George C. Scott**, for "Patton."

10. **James Dean**, for "East of Eden" and "Giant."

11. **Helen Hayes**, 1931-1932's Best Actress (for "The Sin of Madelon Claudet") and 1970's Best Supporting Actress (for "Airport").

12. **Shelley Winters**, for "The Diary of Anne Frank" and "A Patch of Blue."

13. **Barry Fitzgerald**, whose "Going My Way" performance won him both a Best Supporting Actor nomination and the Best Supporting Actor Oscar. He lost in the Best Actor category to his co-star, Bing Crosby.

14. **Peter O'Toole** as King Henry II (in "Becket" and "The Lion in Winter").

15. **King Henry VIII**, an Oscar-winning role for Charles Laughton in "The Private Life of Henry VIII" and a nominated role for both Robert Shaw in "A Man for All Seasons" and Richard Burton in "Anne of the Thousand Days."

16. **Luise Rainer** (for "The Great Ziegfeld" in 1936 and "The Good Earth" in 1937). Her consecutive-win distinction was matched a year later by Spencer Tracy (for "Captains Courageous" in 1937 and "Boys Town" in 1938) and three decades later by Katharine Hepburn (for "Guess Who's Coming to Dinner" in 1967 and "The Lion in Winter" in 1968).

17. **1968** (Katharine Hepburn for "The Lion in Winter" and Barbra Streisand for "Funny Girl").

18. **1931-32** (Wallace Beery for "The Champ" and Fredric March for "Dr. Jekyll and Mr. Hyde").

19. **John Mills**, for "Ryan's Daughter." On the distaff side, two actresses have brought off the same feat: Jane Wyman in "Johnny Belinda" and Patty Duke in "The Miracle Worker."

20. **Sophia Loren's**, in "Two Women."

21. **"Hamlet,"** in 1948.

22. **Robert Wise**, for "West Side Story" and "The Sound of Music."

23. **"Cimarron,"** 1930-31's Best Picture.

24. **"Marty,"** by Paddy Chayefsky.

25. **"Gigi,"** with: Best Picture, Best Director (Vincente Minnelli), Best Screenplay (Alan Jay Lerner), Best Song ("Gigi," by Alan Jay Lerner and Frederick Loewe), Best Scoring of a Musical Picture (Andre Previn), Best Cinematography (Joseph Ruttenberg), Best Film Editing (Adrienne Fazan), Best Art Direction and Set Decoration (William A. Horning and Preston Ames, Henry Grace and Keogh Gleason) and Best Costume Design (Cecil Beaton), plus an honorary Oscar for Maurice Chevalier.

26. **"A Streetcar Named Desire,"** with three Oscared performances (Vivien Leigh's, Karl Malden's and Kim Hunter's).

27. **"Mutiny on the Bounty,"** with three Actor nominees (Clark Gable, Charles Laughton and Franchot Tone). Their only competition, Victor McLaglen in "The Informer," won.

28. **"It Happened One Night"** (Clark Gable and Claudette Colbert).

29. **Clark Gable**, with starring assignments in three Oscar-winning Best Pictures ("It Happened One Night," "Mutiny on the Bounty" and "Gone with the Wind").

30. **Orson Welles**, whose "Citizen Kane" won him nominations for Best Actor and Best Director and the Oscar for Best Original Screenplay (co-authored by Herman J. Mankiewicz).

31. **Ruth Gordon** ("Rosemary's Baby"), Margaret Rutherford ("The V.I.P.s") and Edmund Gwenn ("Miracle on 34th Street") all won Supporting Oscars at the age of 72.

32. **Edith Evans** (80 at the time of her Best Supporting Actress nomination for "The Whisperers").

33. **Patty Duke** (16 at the time of her Best Actress nomination for "The Miracle Worker").

34. **Jackie Cooper** (10 at the time of his Best Actor nomination for "Skippy").

35. **Hattie McDaniel**, for "Gone with the Wind."

36. **Joan Fontaine** ("Suspicion"), Olivia de Havilland ("To Each His Own," "The Heiress").

37. **Lionel Barrymore** ("A Free Soul") and Ethel Barrymore ("None But the Lonely Heart").

38. **Laurence Olivier** ("Hamlet") and Vivien Leigh ("Gone with the Wind" and "A Streetcar Named Desire").

39. **"Treasure of the Sierra Madre"** (supporting actor Walter Huston and screenwriter-director John Huston).

and they really extend their performances.''

On the set, Mars fluffed a line and complained he was having difficulty remembering. Miss Davis retorted, ''When you are 65 years old [like me], you have to remember everything. But I have always been good about learning lines. I could always remember them, and, please God, I always will.'' Then she knocked on wood.

Somebody remarked at lunch about childhood influencing the present. Miss Davis grimaced. ''If it has anything to do with going back to your childhood, I won't have anything to do with it. Yesterday is as far back as I care to go.''

She attacked her salad as if she had just discovered food, then demanded that the waitress come back. ''Get me the recipe for this marvelous salad,'' she said, and then switched to other subjects. ''The trouble these days is, there is no enthusiasm any more. It's a bore to watch people pretend to be bored. Why do they bother? Whatever I do, I do with all my heart.''

Most of the cast were timid in her presence, but only at first. Mars admits, ''I kept turning around and looking at her and saying to myself, 'That's Bette Davis, that's really Bette Davis.'

But she was wonderful. Listen, I've worked with a lot of rotten actors and actresses, so when I tell you I fell in love with her, I mean it. What was amazing to me was here was this sharp, hip, strong lady—and then I discovered she is marshmallow inside. It was such a surprise. There are some personal experiences with her I would never tell anyone because they mean too much to me, but it knocked me out when we'd finish a scene, and if she liked it she'd say, 'Kid, you're the nuts.' I really value her friendship. At the end of shooting we had a small cast party and I felt overcome with a kind of love for her. I have the feeling she sensed my emotions because she turned to me and grinned and said, 'Listen, kid, if this series goes two years, you'll get to love me.' She knocked me out.''

And she may knock out a whole legion of viewers when ''Hello Mother, Goodbye'' turns up on NBC later this season. (END)

—Laddie Marshack

Miss Davis with show's director Peter Hunt.

Test Your OO
(Oscar Quotient)

By Harry Haun

Footnotes are forever being added to Academy Award history. Here is a quiz incorporating 44 years of distinction, large and small. Two points for each correct answer.

1. The most Oscared actress.
2. The most Oscared actor.
3. The most Oscared director.
4. The most Oscared picture (excluding honorary Oscars).
5. The most nominated actress.
6. The most nominated actor.
7. The most nominated director.
8. The most nominated picture.
9. The only performer to refuse the Oscar.
10. The only performer posthumously nominated twice.
11. The only performer Oscared in both starring and supporting categories.
12. The only performer Oscared twice in the Best Supporting Actress category.
13. The only performer nominated twice for the same picture.
14. The only performer nominated twice for the same role in different pictures.
15. The role that has put the greatest number of performers in the Oscar running.
16. The first performer to win two consecutive Oscars.
17. The year of the only Best Actress Oscar tie.
18. The year of the only Best Actor Oscar tie.
19. The only actor to win an Oscar without a single line of dialogue.
20. The only foreign-language performance to win an acting Oscar.

21. The first picture not made in America to win the Best Picture Oscar.
22. The only director Oscared twice for musical pictures.
23. The only Western to win the Best Picture Oscar.
24. The only teleplay to be turned into an Oscar-winning Best Picture.
25. The picture that won an unprecedented nine Oscars out of nine nominations (and also had a performer who received an honorary Oscar the same year).
26. The picture with the greatest number of Oscar-winning performances.
27. The picture with the greatest number of Best Actor nominees.
28. The only picture with Oscared performances from its male and female leads.
29. The performer top-starred in the greatest number of Oscar-winning Best Pictures.
30. The only Oscar-winning screenwriter nominated for acting and directing.
31. The oldest performers to win Oscars.
32. The oldest performer to win an Oscar nomination.
33. The youngest performer to win an Oscar.
34. The youngest performer to win an Oscar nomination.
35. The first black performer to win an Oscar.
36. The only Oscar-winning performers who were sisters.
37. The only Oscar-winning performers who were brother and sister.
38. The only Oscar-winning performers who were husband and wife.
39. The picture that won Oscars for a father and son.

9. An American tourist who falls in love with Rossano Brazzi while in Venice.

10. A champion athlete who is managed by a lowbrow promoter, played by Tracy.

11. An aspiring actress living with several other youngsters, including Ginger Rogers, Eve Arden, Ann Miller, and Lucille Ball.

12. The widow of an American hero who is ultimately discovered (by Tracy) to have been a fascist.

13. A young woman named Sydney Fairchild, in her film debut, in which John Barrymore played her father.

14. A cool, strong-minded socialite named Tracy Lord who remarries her ex-husband, Cary Grant.

15. Herself in one of those awful, all-star wartime efforts in which the stars mixed with soldiers and their girls.

16. The wife of presidential candidate Tracy.

17. Hecuba in a Greek tragedy which co-starred her with Vanessa Redgrave, Irene Papas, and Genevieve Bujold.

18. The vengeful mother of a dead young man named Sebastian Venable in the film version of a Tennessee Williams play.

19. A Chinese peasant in a less than convincing performance, alongside such other Oriental favorites as Walter Huston, Aline MacMahon, Akim Tamiroff, and Agnes Moorehead.

20. A queen imprisoned by another queen, Elizabeth I.

Answers on page 134.

BEST PICTURE AND DIRECTOR
QUIZ NUMBER TWO

1. This man received nominations for his direction of two films which may stand as Hollywood's definitive study of the Mafia.
   a. Name the director.
   b. Name the films.
   c. Name the movie for which he won.

2. This Englishman, whose stage and film career has often been associated with the works of playwright John Osborne, won an Oscar for his extravagantly high-spirited direction of a Henry Fielding novel.
   a. Name the director.
   b. Name the movie.
   c. Name the landmark "angry young man" play that he directed on stage and screen, with Richard Burton starring in the film version.

3. Another British director has twice been honored by the Academy. The first time was for a film dealing with a misguided project by English soldiers in a Japanese prisoner-of-war camp. The second was for a lavish film about a most enigmatic Englishman, which introduced Peter O'Toole in the title role.
   a. Name the director.
   b. Name the two films.
   c. Name the Oscar-winning actor who appeared in both these films.

    d. This same actor was also in two earlier films made by this director, both adaptations of Dickens novels. Name the two films.

4. The story of New York City's efforts to track down those responsible for smuggling heroin into this country became an exciting Oscar-winning film.
    a. Name the picture.
    b. Name the director.
    c. Name the later thriller this director made about a child possessed by the devil.

5. Perhaps the last major musical from the incomparable MGM was this film about a young Parisienne who is trained by her aunts to become a courtesan.
    a. Name the film.
    b. Name the director.
    c. Name those actors in the film who were nominated for their performances.

6. Bogart, Bergman, and Henreid starred in one of the most popular of all films, Warner Brothers' enormously entertaining wartime melodrama.
    a. Name the film.
    b. Name the director.
    c. Who played the urbane Captain Louis Renault, the villainous Major Strasser, and the fez-topped Senor Ferrari?
    d. Who, as the immortal Sam, sang and played "As Time Goes By"?

7. A film about a young man who goes to New York to become a hustler and befriends a crippled outcast named Ratso Rizzo won the Best Picture and Director Oscars.
   a. Name the film.
   b. Name the director.
   c. Name the actor who played the title role.

8. This director's first award was for a film that did not win the Best Picture award (see Best Director quiz). His second Academy Award (1932–33) was for a film that *did* win that Oscar. It was based on a play by Noel Coward and starred Clive Brook and Diana Wynyard.
   a. Name the director.
   b. Name the film.

9. This memorable film about enlisted men—and their women— in Hawaii at the time of the Japanese attack on Pearl Harbor was the first of two films for which its director was honored.
   a. Name the film.
   b. Name the director.
   c. Name three of the stars, all nominated for their performances, who did not win Academy Awards.

10. The second film for which this same director won was markedly different in style and content. It was the screen version of a play by Robert Bolt, the story of an English historical figure who valued his conscience more than his life and was found guilty of treason and executed.
   a. Name the film.
   b. Name the character who was the central figure.
   c. Name the king with whom he fatally clashed.

11. Name the films made by the director in questions 9 and 10 in which:
   a. Gary Cooper won his second Oscar in one of the best of all Westerns.
   b. Gordon MacRae and Shirley Jones starred in the film version of a Rodgers and Hammerstein musical.
   c. Montgomery Clift was first nominated for an Academy Award as a soldier.
   d. Audrey Hepburn made a heroic attempt to give her life to the church.

12. Both Paul Newman–Robert Redford films were directed by the same man. The second film, an entertainment about two con men, was so effective that it became not only an Oscar-winning film but also a box-office bonanza.
   a.   Name the movie.
   b.   Name the director.
   c.   Name the actor who co-starred as Newman and Redford's chief victim.

13. The second film for which this man was named Best Director was also selected as Best Picture. It was the story of two priests, the older, firmly set in his ways, pitted against the younger, who was better able to deal with some of the realities that faced them both.
   a.   Name the film.
   b.   Name the director.

14. The director of this Academy Award winner about a complex World War II general accepted his Oscar, although the star did not.
   a.   Name the movie.
   b.   Name the director.

15. An English musical by Lionel Bart, based on a Dickens novel, was successfully transferred to the screen, directed by someone usually associated with more somber enterprises.
   a.   Name the film.
   b.   Name the director.
   c.   Name the lad who played the title role.

16. Name the memorable thrillers made by the foregoing director which featured:

    a. Orson Welles in postwar Vienna and a haunting musical theme played on a zither.

    b. Ralph Richardson as a butler who is unwittingly destroyed by a young boy who worships him.

    c. James Mason on the lam in Ireland.

17. A harsh and uncompromising film about an alcoholic won the first of two awards for its director.

    a. Name the film.

    b. Name the director.

18. This same director and his film won top honors a second time for a comedy-drama in which one C. C. Baxter is in love with elevator operator Fran Kubelik, who attempts suicide in Baxter's apartment after a final rendezvous with an executive of the company for whom both she and Baxter work.

    a. Name the film.

    b. Name the performers who played C. C. Baxter and Fran Kubelik.

    c. Name the actor who played the executive.

19. Name the films made by the director in questions 17 and 18 in which:

    a. Gloria Swanson made a spectacular return to the screen as a silent-era movie star living in the past.

    b. The classic fade-out line was Joe E. Brown's "Nobody's perfect."

    c. An amoral wife dupes an insurance salesman into helping her murder her husband.

    d. Three Academy Award winners starred in a comedy about a chauffeur's daughter.

20. Three directors contributed to David O. Selznick's most famous film.

    a. Name the film.

    b. Name the director who received sole credit and the Academy Award.

    c. Name the other two directors.

Answers on page 134.

BEST ACTRESS
QUIZ NUMBER ONE

1. Only once—in 1968—has there been a tie vote for Best Actress. Name the actresses and the films for which they won.

2. Name the only actress who has won three Academy Awards for Best Actress and the films for which she won.

3. In addition to the actress just described, one other has won in consecutive years. Name her and the two films for which she won.

4. Several actresses have won the Best Actress award for their screen debut or for their first starring role. Name the actresses who won for portraying:
   a. A runaway princess.
   b. The slatternly wife of an alcoholic.
   c. A talented youngster who became a great Broadway singer-comedienne.
   d. A young French girl who became a saint.
   e. A coldhearted nurse in a mental hospital.

5. In 1950 it appeared to be a toss-up between Bette Davis (*All About Eve*) and Gloria Swanson (*Sunset Boulevard*). Who won?

6. In some cases Oscars are apparently awarded to performers for films following a year in which they did not win the award but it was felt by many that they should have. Bette Davis and Joan Fontaine are two examples.

   a. Name the 1935 and 1941 films for which Davis and Fontaine, respectively, won awards.

   b. Name the earlier films for which each did not win.

7. As noted, Bette Davis won the 1935 Best Actress Oscar. Between 1935 and 1939, Davis and one other actress were the sole winners in that category. Name the winning actresses for 1936, 1937, and 1938.

8. Playing the title role in one of her many rags-to-riches melodramas, Joan Crawford won for her first film at Warner Brothers after many years at MGM.

   a. Name the film.

   b. Name at least three other movies (excluding silent films) in which she played the title role.

9. Jennifer Jones won for a religious film in which she played the title role.

   a. Name the film.

   b. Name at least three other movies in which she played the title role.

10. Miss Jones was also nominated for her performances as:

   a. A girl in love with a soldier, who was played by her first husband, Robert Walker (a Best Supporting Actress nomination).

   b. The fiery half-breed Pearl Chavez in an overripe Western.

   c. A young woman who lost her memory and is known only as Singleton.

   d. A Eurasian who falls in love with an American.

11. Grace Kelly won a Best Actress award in the nonglamorous role of Georgie Elgin, the wife of an alcoholic actor.

   a. Name the picture.

   b. Name a film, which starred Clark Gable and Ava Gardner, for which she was nominated as Best Supporting Actress.

12. Miss Kelly, before leaving films to become Princess Grace of Monaco, co-starred in three Hitchcock films.

   a. Name the three movies.

   b. Name her leading man in each.

13. Faye Dunaway received an Oscar on her third nomination, winning as a neurotically driven television executive.
    a. Name the film for which she won.
    b. Name an earlier film for which she was nominated.

14. This actress played many fluffy ingenue roles before she began to give some emotionally complex, powerful performances, including her Oscar-winning work as a tart-tongued hooker named Bree Daniels.
    a. Name this actress.
    b. Name the movie.
    c. Name the actor who played the title role.

15. Name the film for which this same actress won an earlier nomination for her strong performance as a participant in a grueling dance marathon.

16. Susan Hayward received five Oscar nominations. Among the characters she portrayed were actress Lillian Roth, singer Jane Froman, and convicted murderess Barbara Graham.
    a. Name the movies in which she portrayed these women.
    b. Name the movie for which she won her Academy Award.
    c. Name her two earlier Oscar-nominated performances.

17. In one of the major upsets in Academy Award history, this dependable leading lady won for her spirited performance as a Swedish maid who goes into politics.
   a. Name the actress.
   b. Name the film.
   c. Name her leading man, a reliable presence in several Selznick films.

18. No actress had ever been honored for a performance in a foreign-language film until this voluptuous actress won for her portrayal of an Italian mother who is a victim (as is her daughter) of war and rape.
   a. Name the actress.
   b. Name the film.

19. Another Italian actress, famed for the passionate, explosive emotions she brought to her work, won the Oscar for her first American film, adapted from a play Tennessee Williams had written for her.
   a. Name the actress.
   b. Name the film.
   c. Name another film, also adapted from a Williams play, in which she co-starred with Marlon Brando and Joanne Woodward.
   d. Name the actress who created both of these roles on Broadway and consented to play a supporting role in the Brando–Woodward film.

20. For years Warner Brothers cast this actress in secondary, lightweight roles in comedies. Proving her dramatic abilities on loanouts to other studios, she returned to Warners and won her award for touchingly playing a deaf-mute who is raped.
   a. Name the actress.
   b. Name her winning film.
   c. Name the two loan-out movies in which she scored, the first at Paramount with Ray Milland and the second at MGM with Gregory Peck.

Answers on page 136.

1939

This quiz concentrates on films released during the vintage year of 1939.

1. Name the three actresses who were nominated for Academy Awards for *Gone With the Wind*.

2. Name the performers in *Gone With the Wind* who played:
   a. Prissy
   b. Belle Watling
   c. Aunt Pittypat
   d. Doctor Meade
   e. Scarlett's two sisters

3. Although *Gone With the Wind* won the Best Picture Oscar, it lost the New York Film Critics' Award to another film that was produced by Samuel Goldwyn and directed by William Wyler.
   a. Name the other film.
   b. Name four of its leading players.

4. Clark Gable's performance as Rhett Butler brought him a Best Actor nomination, but he lost the Oscar to a British actor who played a dedicated teacher.
   a. Name the winning actor.
   b. Name the film for which he won.

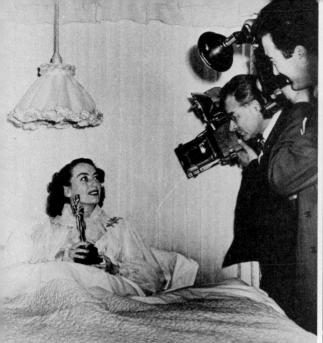

5. In addition to playing Scarlett O'Hara's father, Gerald O'Hara, Thomas Mitchell appeared in several other major films in 1939.
  a. Name the two films he appeared in with Jean Arthur.
  b. Name the film he played in with Charles Laughton and Maureen O'Hara.
  c. Name the film for which he won the Oscar for Best Supporting Actor.

6. One of Hollywood's finest achievements, *The Wizard of Oz*, won the Academy Award for Best Musical Score and, of course, made a star of Judy Garland. Name the actors who played:
  a. the title role
  b. the scarecrow
  c. the tin man
  d. the lion
  e. the wicked witch
  f. Glinda, the good witch
  g. Auntie Em

7. *Mr. Smith Goes to Washington* boasted a Who's Who of Hollywood's character actors in its supporting cast. Name at least three of these actors.

8. One of the screen's finest character actresses received her only nomination for her performance in a film set in the earliest days of the republic, a movie that starred Claudette Colbert and Henry Fonda.

    a. Name the actress.

    b. Name the film.

    c. Name another film released during this year in which she appeared with Astaire and Rogers in their penultimate film.

    d. Name the films in which she memorably played Aunt March and Aunt Betsey.

9. Name at least four performers who were in John Ford's peerless Western, *Stagecoach*.

10. Name the film in which Don Ameche played his most famous role as a great American inventor.

11. Name at least four actresses in the star-laden cast of *The Women*.

12. Ingrid Bergman made her American debut in a film she had earlier made in Swedish.

    a. Name the film.

    b. Name her co-star.

13. Cary Grant, Victor McLaglen, and Douglas Fairbanks, Jr., starred in a rousing adventure story inspired by a Rudyard Kipling poem.

    a. Name the movie.

    b. Name the actor who played the title role.

14. Nominated for another film, James Stewart also played the title role in a highly amusing Western that teamed him with Marlene Dietrich.
   a.   Name the film.
   b.   Name the song Dietrich sang, which has become one of those most closely associated with her.

15. Bette Davis was especially active in 1939. Name the films in which she appeared with:
   a.   Errol Flynn and Olivia de Havilland
   b.   Miriam Hopkins
   c.   Humphrey Bogart and Ronald Reagan

16. Greta Garbo won her last Oscar nomination in one of her most popular films, a comedy directed by the incomparable Ernst Lubitsch.
   a.   Name the movie.
   b.   Name the Broadway star who made one of her few motion-picture appearances as the Grand Duchess Swana.
   c.   Name the only film Garbo later starred in.

17. This "let's-put-on-a-show!" film garnered a Best Actor nomination for its star (appearing opposite Judy Garland), although it was probably more of a tribute to his tremendous box-office popularity than to the demands the movie made upon his considerable talents.
   a. Name the actor.
   b. Name the film.
   c. Name the character he played in the series with which he is most closely associated.
   d. Name the actors who played his father, mother, and sister in the above-mentioned series.

18. Geraldine Fitzgerald gave superior performances in both *Dark Victory* and *Wuthering Heights*. For which of these films did she receive a Best Supporting Actress nomination?

19. Irene Dunne received one of her five Best Actress nominations starring opposite Charles Boyer in a four-handkerchief romantic drama directed by Leo McCarey.
   a. Name the movie.
   b. Name the noted Russian character actress nominated for her supporting performance in this film.
   c. Name at least two other films for which Miss Dunne was nominated.

20. Name the 1939 films in which the following actors appeared:
   a. Clark Gable and Norma Shearer
   b. Burgess Meredith, Betty Field, and Lon Chaney, Jr.
   c. Carole Lombard and James Stewart
   d. Tyrone Power and Henry Fonda
   e. Edward G. Robinson, Francis Lederer, and George Sanders
   f. Myrna Loy, Tyrone Power, and George Brent
   g. Henry Fonda and Alice Brady
   h. Bob Hope and Paulette Goddard
   i. Barbara Stanwyck and William Holden
   j. Spencer Tracy, Nancy Kelly, and Sir Cedric Hardwicke

Answers on page 137.

BEST ACTRESS
QUIZ NUMBER TWO

1. A durable star of the thirties and forties, she moved from comedy to drama with apparent ease. She was honored for a comedy in which she played a runaway heiress who falls for a reporter.
    a. Name the actress.
    b. Name the film.
    c. Name the wartime soap opera for which she was nominated, a story about the families the soldiers left behind, which David O. Selznick typically turned into an all-star extravaganza.

2. Well known not only as a major talent in her own right but also as the wife of a famous star, she won an Oscar for her expert performance as a woman with multiple personalities.
    a. Name the actress.
    b. Name the picture.
    c. Name the movie for which she was nominated in which she played a drab, lonely schoolteacher, a film directed by her husband.

3. The reigning queen of MGM during the war years was a beautiful redhead, whose genteel manners and British accent served her well. One of the more noble heroines she portrayed was the title character in a timely film about a brave English family surviving air raids and other traumas.
    a. Name the actress.

b.   Name this film for which she won her award.

c.   Name the actor who starred opposite her in this and several other films.

4. As did Bette Davis, the actress in the preceding question received five consecutive Best Actress nominations, hers running from 1941 through 1945.

a.   Name the films that earned her nominations, excluding the movie for which she won in 1942.

b.   Name the earlier film for which she was nominated, playing the wife of Robert Donat.

c.   Name the later film for which she was nominated, playing a famous First Lady.

5. As a bright, tough, world-weary housekeeper to rancher Melvyn Douglas and his two sons, this actress deservedly won the Oscar for what was actually a secondary role.

a.   Name the actress.

b.   Name the movie.

c.   Name the actor who played the title role of one of Douglas's sons.

6. This actress was honored for her radiant title performance as a young widow who travels through the Southwest with her precocious son, with unwarranted hopes of becoming a singer.

a.   Name the actress.

b.   Name the movie.

c.   Name the actor who played her romantic interest.

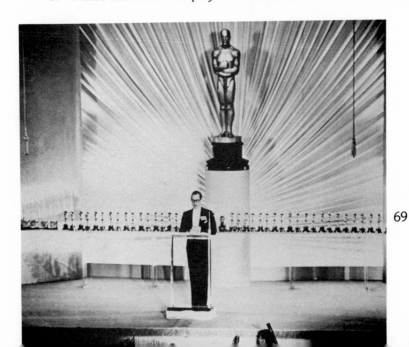

7. This same actress received an earlier Best Actress nomination, vying for the award as a movie star whose daughter shows increasingly disturbing behavior.
   a. Name the film.
   b. Name the young actress who played her unfortunate daughter.
   c. Name the actor who played the title role.

8. This English actress won her award as a reckless, "with-it" young woman in a film that dealt with an assortment of characters (two of whom played by Dirk Bogarde and Laurence Harvey) who supposedly typified "swinging London" in the sixties.
   a. Name the actress.
   b. Name the picture.
   c. Name the lavish film in which she portrayed Lara, a Russian girl whose name is associated with the movie's famous musical theme.

9. One of the finest comediennes of recent years, this British actress also has impressive dramatic skills, proving it with an Oscar-winning performance as a complex and neurotic teacher who imposes her unorthodox views on her students.
   a. Name the actress.
   b. Name the film.
   c. Name the Shakespearean movie, for which she received a Best Supporting Actress nomination, in which she played the wife of Laurence Olivier.

10. As Sally Bowles in the musical version of Christopher Isherwood's stories about Berlin in the early thirties, this actress-singer scored triumphantly.
   a. Name the actress.
   b. Name the movie.
   c. Name the actor with whom she co-starred.

11. The first Academy Award for Best Actress went to a delicate star who was honored for not one but three performances, in *Seventh Heaven*, *Street Angel*, and *Sunrise*.
   a. Name the actress.
   b. Name the Selznick movie about Hollywood in which she

starred as a rising young actress married to an actor whose career is declining.

   c.   Name another Selznick film in which she, Douglas Fairbanks, Jr., Billie Burke, and Roland Young were happy-go-lucky thieves.

12. "America's Sweetheart" of the silent era came out of retirement and won the second Best Actress Oscar for playing a southern lass.

   a.   Name the actress.
   b.   Name the film for which she won.

13. She enjoyed regal status at MGM, along with Garbo, partly because she happened to be married to the studio's production chief. She won an Oscar playing the title role in one of her earliest sound films.

   a.   Name the actress.
   b.   Name the film for which she won.
   c.   Name the head of production to whom she was married.

14. Naturally, many plum roles came the way of the actress just described. Name the films in which she:

   a.   Starred opposite Robert Montgomery in the film version of a Noel Coward play.
   b.   Sported a blond wig and a phony Russian accent in the film version of a play by Robert Sherwood.
   c.   Had malicious friends and an unfaithful husband in the film version of a play by Clare Boothe Luce.
   d.   Starred opposite Leslie Howard in the film version of a play by Shakespeare, in which both performers were rather mature for their roles.

15. This actress had to leave Hollywood for Broadway to prove her worth. She was honored for re-creating her stage success as Annie Sullivan, the patient teacher of a deaf, dumb, and blind girl.

   a.   Name the actress.
   b.   Name the film.
   c.   Name another film in which she played a seductive "older woman" whose name has become famous from a Simon and Garfunkel song.

16. A long-time comedienne in silents, this hefty actress became a major star at the end of her career. She teamed up raucously with Wallace Beery for her Oscar-winning performance.
    a. Name the actress.
    b. Name the film.
    c. Name the memorable MGM movie in which she was top-billed as a famous actress named Carlotta Vance.

17. The same year the film version of a great musical was released without her re-creation of her acclaimed Broadway perform-ance, she won an Oscar for another musical.
    a. Name the actress.
    b. Name the movie for which she won.
    c. Name the musical film and the role in it that she had lost.

18. The next year the actress just mentioned starred in one of the great money-making films of all time.
    a. Name the film.
    b. Name the actor who co-starred with her.
    c. Name another musical, in which she appeared with Mary Tyler Moore and Carol Channing.

19. This French actress, noted for her portrayals of disillusioned, worldly-wise women, won her Academy Award opposite an English actor playing a ruthlessly ambitious young man.
    a. Name the actress.
    b. Name the film.
    c. Name the actor with whom she co-starred.

20. Name Stanley Kramer's all-star film for which the foregoing ac-tress was nominated, in which she played La Condesa opposite Oskar Werner in some luminously sensitive love scenes.

Answers on page 139.

BEST SONG

1. Match the Oscar-winning song with the movie in which it was sung.

a. "It Might As Well Be Spring"

b. "White Christmas"

c. "High Hopes"

d. "The Shadow of Your Smile"

e. "On the Atchison, Topeka and Santa Fe"

f. "Que Sera, Sera"

g. "The Continental"

h. "Buttons and Bows"

i. "In the Cool, Cool, Cool of the Evening"

j. "Lullaby of Broadway"

k. "When You Wish Upon a Star"

l. "Zip-a-Dee-Doo-Dah"

m. "Swinging on a Star"

n. "Thanks for the Memory"

o. "For All We Know"

1. *Lovers and Other Strangers*

2. *Song of the South*

3. *Pinocchio*

4. *Going My Way*

5. *Gold Diggers of 1935*

6. *Holiday Inn*

7. *The Big Broadcast of 1938*

8. *State Fair*

9. *The Gay Divorcee*

10. *The Sandpiper*

11. *The Paleface*

12. *The Harvey Girls*

13. *Here Comes the Groom*

14. *The Man Who Knew Too Much*

15. *A Hole in the Head*

2. Match the Oscar-winning song with the performer(s) with whom it is associated.

a.	"Secret Love"	1.	Bing Crosby
b.	"The Way We Were"	2.	Keith Carradine
c.	"The Way You Look Tonight"	3.	Louis Jourdan
d.	"Over the Rainbow"	4.	Doris Day
e.	"Buttons and Bows"	5.	Fred Astaire and Ginger Rogers
f.	"You'll Never Know"	6.	Frank Sinatra
g.	"Sweet Leilani"	7.	Judy Garland
h.	"All the Way"	8.	Alice Faye
i.	"I'm Easy"	9.	Barbra Streisand
j.	"Gigi"	10.	Bob Hope

3. Match the Oscar-winning song with the composer and lyricist who wrote it.

a. "Mona Lisa"
b. "The Way You Look Tonight"
c. "Baby, It's Cold Outside"
d. "The Last Time I Saw Paris"
e. "High Noon"
f. "Three Coins in the Fountain"
g. "Evergreen"
h. "Gigi"
i. "Moon River"
j. "Chim Chim Cher-ee"
k. "Never on Sunday"
l. "Love Is a Many-Splendored Thing"
m. "It Might As Well Be Spring"
n. "The Windmills of Your Mind"
o. "Raindrops Keep Fallin' on My Head"

1. Burt Bacharach and Hal David
2. Jerome Kern and Dorothy Fields
3. Richard Rodgers and Oscar Hammerstein II
4. Richard M. Sherman and Robert B. Sherman
5. Frank Loesser
6. Sammy Fain and Paul Francis Webster
7. Jerome Kern and Oscar Hammerstein II
8. Dimitri Tiomkin and Ned Washington
9. Jule Styne and Sammy Cahn
10. Michel Legrand and Alan and Marilyn Bergman
11. Barbra Streisand and Paul Williams
12. Frederick Loewe and Alan Jay Lerner
13. Henry Mancini and Johnny Mercer
14. Ray Evans and Jay Livingston
15. Manos Hadjidakis

Answers on page 141.

BEST SUPPORTING ACTOR

QUIZ NUMBER ONE

1. Name at least one of the films for which Walter Brennan won an Academy Award.

2. He was the only actor ever nominated for Best Actor and Best Supporting Actor for the same role, winning in the latter category.
    a.   Name the actor.
    b.   Name the movie.
    c.   To whom did he lose the Best Actor award?

3. Having been given a special award for his performance, he also won the Oscar for Best Supporting Actor, thus becoming the only person honored twice for the same role.
    a.   Name the actor.
    b.   Name the film.

4. He worked with Orson Welles in the theater, produced such films as *The Bad and the Beautiful* and *Executive Suite*, and in his seventies won an Oscar for his performance as a frosty college professor.
    a.   Name the actor.
    b.   Name the film.
    c.   Name the young actor who played the leading role of his student.

5. He won for portraying Ben Bradlee of the *Washington Post*, the paper credited for breaking open the Watergate scandal.

    a. Name the actor.
    b. Name the film.
    c. Name the actor who starred in and produced the film.

6. Name the actor who won for playing a man who may or may not have been Santa Claus.

7. Name the films in which the actor just mentioned:
    a. Fell from the top of a building as he tried to push Joel McCrea to his death.
    b. Was the father of, among others, Greer Garson, Maureen O'Sullivan, and Marsha Hunt.
    c. Played the title role of a counterfeiter.

8. Three actors were nominated in the Best Supporting Actor category for *On the Waterfront* and both *Godfather* films.
    a. Name the actors nominated for *On the Waterfront*.
    b. Name the actors nominated for *The Godfather Part II*.
    c. Which, if any, of the above six actors won?

9. An urbane leading man in his younger days, he developed into a solid character actor and won his award as a small-town rancher with two sons who were played by Paul Newman and Brandon de Wilde.
    a. Name the actor.
    b. Name the picture.
    c. Name an earlier movie in which he romanced the great Garbo in Paris.

10. Infrequently cast in heroic roles, he seemed more at home playing cads, weaklings, and Nazis. In his finest (and Oscar-winning) performance he played a Broadway drama critic.
    a. Name the actor.
    b. Name the film.
    c. Name either the character he played or the actual critic on whom the character was based.

11. Many years before his memorable stage and screen performances as Anne Frank's father, this actor was honored for portraying an innocent French officer whose imprisonment became a *cause célèbre*.

a. Name the actor.
b. Name the movie.
c. Name the actress who played his warm and loyal wife.

12. Famed for his girth and gentlemanly villainy, he made a spectacular film debut in a classic 1941 melodrama and received his only Oscar nomination.
a. Name the actor.
b. Name the picture.
c. Name the diminutive actor he appeared with, who was later to act with him in several films during the forties.

13. A far cry, indeed, from Pip in *Great Expectations* was the bizarre character—a sort of village idiot—for which this actor won his Oscar.
a. Name the actor.
b. Name the film.
c. Name his daughter who won a special Oscar for a Walt Disney film.

14. This great actor was nominated four times for an Academy Award, although he never won. His nominations were for portraying a brilliant but compromised United States senator, a suave, amoral French officer in North Africa, a Jewish businessman married to a vain woman, and a pawn in an international intrigue who discovers he is married to a spy.
a. Name the actor.
b. Name the four films for which he was nominated.

15. In one of the preceding films this same actor appeared opposite Bette Davis. In two other superior performances he played Davis's omnipotent doctor and a temperamental composer who was her lover. Name the two films.

16. Well before his name became a fixture in those all-star cast lists for Universal "disaster" movies, he won an Oscar for playing a brutal oppressor of Paul Newman.
a. Name the actor.
b. Name the film.

17. Re-creating his stage success, this versatile performer won an Oscar for having somehow managed to be immensely enter-

taining in his musical numbers, while simultaneously epitomizing evil, corruption, and sleazy amorality.
   a. Name the actor.
   b. Name the movie.

18. He and Charles Bickford were bitter enemies in the William Wyler Western for which he won his award. Among his co-stars were Gregory Peck, Jean Simmons, and Charlton Heston.
   a. Name the actor.
   b. Name the film.
   c. Name another film, adapted from a play by Tennessee Williams, in which he re-created his most famous stage role.

19. In a harrowing film about marathon dancers in the thirties, this actor won for his performance as the seedy master of ceremonies.
   a. Name the actor.
   b. Name the movie.
   c. Name two other performers in the film.

20. "Damn the torpedoes, full speed ahead!" was his motto in his Oscar-winning role as matchmaking Mr. Dingle, sharing a flat in overcrowded wartime Washington with a young woman and a young man.
   a. Name the actor.
   b. Name the film.
   c. Name his two co-stars.
   d. Name the richly textured, somber Warner Brothers melodrama in which he played a sadistic doctor who needlessly mutilated Ronald Reagan.

Answers on page 141.

SPENCER TRACY

Name the films in which Spencer Tracy:

1. Played a Portuguese fisherman named Manuel.

2. First portrayed Father Flanagan.

3. Played Aubrey Piper in the title role of a film, his first for MGM, that was based on a play by George Kelly.

4. Made his only screen appearance with Bette Davis, a movie that was later remade under another title with John Garfield and Ann Sheridan.

5. Searched for Sir Cedric Hardwicke in Africa and uttered four memorable words when he found him.

6. Portrayed perhaps the most famous of all American inventors.

7. Played a priest, appearing with Clark Gable and Jeanette MacDonald.

8. Played Clark Gable's friend and rival in a story about fortunes made and lost in the oil business, a movie that also starred Claudette Colbert and Hedy Lamarr.

9. Appeared with Gable and Myrna Loy in a film about aviation.

10. Accepted second billing for the last time in a film with Gable.

11. Said of Katharine Hepburn, "There's not much meat on her, but what's there is 'cherce.'"

12. Visited a small, unfriendly place that was populated with such Academy Award winners as Ernest Borgnine, Walter Brennan, Dean Jagger, and Lee Marvin.

13. Played Joan Bennett's husband and Elizabeth Taylor's father so successfully that the trio was reunited for a sequel.

14. Played Teresa Wright's husband and Jean Simmons's father in a movie based on Ruth Gordon's autobiographical play.

15. Co-starred with Fredric March and played a lawyer not unlike Clarence Darrow.

16. Starred as a fisherman in a movie based on a Hemingway novella.

17. Portrayed a compassionate American judge at postwar military trials in Germany.

18. Was cast as a Mexican-American, along with Hedy Lamarr, John Garfield, and Frank Morgan, in a movie adapted from a John Steinbeck novel.

19. Played Lieutenant Colonel James H. Doolittle.

20. Made his last screen appearance.

Answers on page 142.

BEST SUPPORTING ACTOR
QUIZ NUMBER TWO

1. His career in Hollywood began many years before sound came along, and this veteran became one of the industry's most dependable character actors, bringing strength and simple dignity to many roles. He won his award as a Welsh coal miner in a highly acclaimed film.
    a. Name the actor.
    b. Name the film.
    c. Name the youngster who played the pivotal role of his youngest son, Huw.

2. A reliable stage and screen character actor for years, his wry delivery and shambling charm brought him stardom on Broadway in a Neil Simon comedy about two recently divorced men. He co-starred in the film version with Jack Lemmon, but won his Oscar earlier for a film in which he played Lemmon's disastrously self-assured brother-in-law.
    a. Name the actor.
    b. Name the film for which he won.
    c. Name the Simon comedy he appeared in with Lemmon.

3. This young actor won an Oscar for an American film, but almost all his dialogue was in Italian.
    a. Name the actor.
    b. Name the film.
    c. Name a film in which he played a dying baseball player.
    d. Name another film in which he played a dangerous character named Travis Bickle.

4. He was nominated for *Champion, Trial, Peyton Place*, and *Some Came Running*, and he received a Best Actor nomination for *Bright Victory*. Name this actor who has yet to win.

5. After having been a Fox leading man, his movie career seemed about over until he made a major comeback as Johnny Nolan, the wayward father in a moving drama of an Irish family in New York in the early 1900s.
   a. Name the actor.
   b. Name the picture.
   c. Name the radiant young actress who played his wife, Katie.

6. He had been a lesser-known member of the "John Ford stock company" for years, appearing primarily in Westerns, until he won an award for his performance in a film set in a small, dusty town, in which the closing of the local movie theater became a symbol of changing times and the town's decay.
   a. Name the actor.
   b. Name the movie.
   c. Name one of the two actors who played the teen-age leading roles.

7. Winning for a postwar film in which he played an air force major, a movie in which Gregory Peck gave one of his strongest performances, this character actor did his most memorable work.
   a. Name the actor.
   b. Name the picture.
   c. Name the unfortunate film, in which he played Helen Hayes's husband, that unwittingly suggested that intelligence and higher education led to becoming a Communist.

8. Appearing as the leader of a Puerto Rican street gang in New York in the film version of the famous musical with a Bernstein-Sondheim score, this actor won an Oscar for the role he had played on the stage.
   a. Name the actor.
   b. Name the film.
   c. Name the actress who played the role of his sister.

9. This veteran comedian returned to the screen after years of radio

and television stardom as straight man to his wife. He played
the mellower half of an old vaudeville team that is briefly reunited, in the screen version of a Neil Simon play.

    a. Name the actor.
    b. Name the film.
    c. Name the actor who co-starred as his ex-partner.

10. This British character actor has never been accused of under-
playing. He was comparatively restrained in his award-winning
role in an MGM—William Wyler biblical spectacular.

    a. Name the actor.
    b. Name the film.
    c. Name the bawdy movie that later won a Best Picture
       Oscar, in which he was nominated for playing a country
       squire.

11. This actor played a sweaty Hollywood agent named Oscar Mul-
doon in a Mankiewicz movie about an uneducated girl who
becomes a glamorous film star.

    a. Name the actor.
    b. Name the film.
    c. Name the actress who played the title role.

12. He created the role of the Irish-American father in an unheralded three-character play that won the Pulitzer Prize. He won an Oscar repeating his role in the film version.
  a. Name the actor.
  b. Name the film.
  c. Name the Oscar-winning actress who was nominated as his wife in the screen version.

13. This actor triumphed as a toothless, wily old gold prospector in one of the best of all American films.
  a. Name the actor.
  b. Name the movie.
  c. Name the film for which he was nominated, years earlier, as Best Actor, in which he portrayed the title character who left his wife, Ruth Chatterton, to find happiness with Mary Astor.

14. Always considered a "New York actor" in spite of his many film appearances, he was honored for playing the well-heeled brother of nonconformist Jason Robards in the film version of Herb Gardner's comedy.
  a. Name the actor.
  b. Name the film.
  c. Name the film in which, in probably his most well-known screen moment, he was fatally stabbed at the top of a staircase.

15. He won for playing "Boss" Finley in the movie version of a Tennessee Williams play. His specialty was portraying men of limited vision, whom time had passed by or who were simply bewildered or bigoted.
  a. Name the actor.
  b. Name the film.
  c. Name the film in which, cast to type, he portrayed an executive being replaced by a younger, abler man, played by Van Heflin.

16. Known as a stage and television comedian, he turned to films and won his award as a GI stationed in Japan who falls in love with a Japanese girl and, with her, commits suicide.
  a. Name the actor.

b. Name the movie.

c. Name the nautical "disaster" film in which he portrayed one of the few survivors.

17. Name the craggy-faced actor who won nominations for his strong performances as a priest in *The Song of Bernadette*, a butler in *The Farmer's Daughter*, and the heroine's father in *Johnny Belinda*.

18. Mitch was a character who desperately needed to escape from his possessive mother. His appearance in this award-winning role was not the only time this actor has been associated with Elia Kazan and Tennessee Williams.
   a. Name the actor.
   b. Name the film.
   c. Name another Williams—Kazan effort in which he was the jealous husband of Carroll Baker.

19. One of the supreme entertainers of our time, he suffered a major setback in mid-career and rebounded magnificently with his portrayal of a doomed soldier in the film version of James Jones's best known novel.
   a. Name the actor.
   b. Name the film.
   c. Name the later movie in which he played a drug addict named Frankie Machine.

20. Among the highest peaks of this same actor's screen career were the three MGM musicals that cast him opposite an actor whose screen persona complemented his perfectly.
   a. Name the other actor.
   b. Name the three musicals in which they co-starred.

Answers on page 143.

BETTE DAVIS

1. Bette Davis's first Oscar, apparently a consolation prize for an earlier acting triumph, has been covered in Best Actress Quiz Number One. Name her second Academy Award–winning film in which she played a tempestuous, nineteenth-century Louisiana belle, a role that is widely considered to be Davis's revenge for not having been cast as Scarlett O'Hara.

2. "Prognosis: negative" was the medical opinion, and a rich, high-spirited Davis began her descent to blindness and death in one of her most moving performances.
   a. Name the film.
   b. Name the British actress who so splendidly played Davis's best friend.
   c. Name the leading man who appeared with her in many films and never got in the way.

3. She and Paul Muni co-starred in a film in which they never appeared together.
   a. Name the movie.
   b. Name the actor who—regardless of the likes of Davis, Muni, Rains, Sondergaard, et al.—walked off with the film and a Best Supporting Actor nomination as Emperor Maximilian von Habsburg.

4. One of her most dismal films, the last under her Warner Brothers contract, was immortalized by her famous line, "What a dump!"

a. Name the film.
b. Name the actor who played her long-suffering husband.
c. Name the famous play and film that opens with a couple discussing the line and the movie.

5. In a film in which we first see her as a vain young woman named Fanny Trellis, Davis was forever breaking luncheon dates with her friend Janie Clarkson.
   a. Name the movie.
   b. Name the performer who played the title role.
   c. Name the performer who played Janie Clarkson.

6. In one of her most beloved weepers, Davis played a frumpy spinster who, transformed into a beauty with the help of Claude Rains and Warners' technicians, finds love in the Caribbean with a man who has a unique way of lighting cigarettes.
   a. Name the film.
   b. Name the actor who lit the cigarettes.
   c. Name the distinguished actress who was nominated as Best Supporting Actress for playing Davis's domineering mother.

7. Davis was particularly nasty to husbands played by Herbert Marshall. In one film she was unfaithful to him and also murdered her lover. In another, a dying Marshall was horrified to watch the merciless Bette silently refuse to fetch his lifesaving medication.
   a. Name the film in which she was unfaithful.
   b. Name the film in which she let Marshall die.
   c. Name at least one performer who was nominated in the supporting category for either of the above films.

8. In perhaps the wittiest of all American screenplays, she hit one of the peaks of her career as a Broadway star who has a director for a lover, a complex about her age, and a scheming secretary.
   a. Name the movie.
   b. Name the actor who played her director-lover (and became her off-screen husband).
   c. Name the actress who played her wisecracking, ex-vaudevillian maid, Birdie Coonan.

9. Except for the foregoing role, she seldom triumphed in comedy.

Nevertheless, Warner Brothers tossed her into three comedies during the forties. Name the pictures in which she co-starred with:

    a. James Cagney
    b. Monty Woolley
    c. Robert Montgomery

10. Name the film, directed by John Huston, in which Davis and de Havilland played the Timberlake sisters whose first names were Stanley and Roy.

11. Name the two films in which she co-starred with Miriam Hopkins.

12. In what later success did a crazed Davis terrorize her paralyzed sister, played by no less than Joan Crawford?

13. Name another shocker in which she was reunited with Olivia de Havilland, Joseph Cotten, and (although they were never in a scene together) Mary Astor.

14. The starring role of the lower-middle-class wife of a Bronx taxi driver in an MGM film seems peculiar territory for Davis, but she gave this part a gallant try. She has been quoted (inaccurately, one hopes) as saying it is her favorite role. Name the movie.

15. In a role Ethel Barrymore created on the stage, Davis played a Welsh schoolteacher who diligently coached a promising young student.
    a. Name the film.
    b. Name the actor who played the student.
    c. Name the actor-playwright who wrote the play.

16. Name the man who directed her in three of her most memorable films: *Jezebel, The Letter,* and *The Little Foxes.*

17. Name the film in which a subdued Davis played the warm, self-sacrificing wife of antifascist Paul Lukas, the role for which he won the Best Actor Oscar.

18. Name the two films in which she portrayed Elizabeth I.

19. Not to be outdone by Paramount's *Star Spangled Rhythm,* Warners drafted all its stars for a patriotic wartime revue, tied to a feeble story featuring Eddie Cantor.
    a. Name the film.
    b. Name the song Davis sang in the movie.

20. In which films did she play the following characters?
    a. Judith Traherne
    b. Margo Channing
    c. Rosa Moline
    d. Regina Giddens
    e. Mildred Rogers
    f. Charlotte Vale
    g. Julie Marston
    h. Gabrielle Maple
    i. Miss Moffat
    j. Leslie Crosbie

Answers on page 145.

BEST SUPPORTING ACTRESS
QUIZ NUMBER ONE

1. A unique and statuesque actress made her screen debut and won the first Best Supporting Actress award for a major Warner Brothers adventure film starring Fredric March.
   a. Name the actress.
   b. Name the film.
   c. Name the comedian she menaced in, among other films, *The Cat and the Canary* and *My Favorite Blonde*.

2. A veteran Broadway star won for portraying a witch living on Manhattan's West Side.
   a. Name the actress.
   b. Name the film.
   c. Name the actress who played her victim.

3. She was an unexpected winner for her strong but brief performance as the wife of a television executive having an affair with a younger woman.
   a. Name the actress.
   b. Name the film.
   c. Name the actor who played her husband.

4. Two women were nominated for Best Supporting Actress for their performances in *Mildred Pierce*. One played Mildred's evil daughter, Veda, and later became an MGM musical star. The other played her trademarked role of the wisecracking, warm-hearted good friend. Name the women.

5. Teresa Wright was nominated as Best Actress and Best Supporting Actress in the same year, winning in the latter category. Name the films for which she was nominated.

6. Two apple-pie girl-next-door types did an about-face, portrayed prostitutes, and won Oscars. Name the actresses and the films for which they won their awards in 1953 and 1960.

7. Which actress who never won an Oscar has more Best Supporting Actress nominations than anyone else?

8. Name at least two of the films for which the foregoing actress was nominated.

9. She was nominated for her first film—in 1951—in which she hilariously portrayed a shoplifter. She has since been nominated three times: as the mother of a landlord, a Beverly Hills matron, and an ill-fated passenger on a German liner.
   a. Name the actress.
   b. Name the 1951 film.
   c. Name the film for which she won an Oscar.
   d. Name at least one of the other films for which she was nominated.

10. Name the Greek actress who was honored for playing the strong-willed Pilar in *For Whom the Bell Tolls*.

11. In this same film the American hero, Robert Jordan, was indeed played by an American, Gary Cooper. However, in addition to the previously mentioned actress, other Spanish characters were played by a Swede, a few Russians, an Italian, and other assorted Europeans. Name at least three of these performers.

12. Dispensing warmth and wisdom, she played the mother of Montgomery Clift, Jennifer Jones, John Garfield, Elizabeth Taylor, and Gregory Peck in various films.
   a. Name the actress.
   b. Name the films in which she played the mother of the performers named.
   c. For which of these films did she win the Oscar?

13. Nineteen forty-one was a banner year at Warner Brothers for her. Playing a concert pianist, she stole a film, almost succeeded

in stealing the inevitable George Brent from Bette Davis, and won an Academy Award.
   a.   Name the actress.
   b.   Name the film.

14. Name the Warners private-eye gem of that same year in which the just-described actress was the less-than-virtuous leading lady.

15. She and Robert Stack were both nominated for their supporting performances in a third-rate Universal melodrama. He lost, she won.
   a.   Name the actress.
   b.   Name the picture.
   c.   Name one of Bogart's better-known films in which she first attracted attention as a bookstore proprietress.
   d.   Name the later film in which she co-starred with Errol Flynn, a show-business biography.

16. In a glossy film about Hollywood that claimed six Academy Awards she won as the fatally flirtatious wife of a screenwriter.
   a.   Name the actress.
   b.   Name the film.
   c.   Name the actor who played her husband.
   d.   Name at least two other co-stars of this MGM film.

17. This same actress was nominated earlier for playing another of her sexy, lippy tarts in a film dealing with anti-Semitism, in which Robert Ryan played the dangerously warped bigot.
   a.   Name the movie.
   b.   This film boasted three stars with the same first name. Who were Ryan's co-stars?

18. She played Charles Foster Kane's mother and won the New York Film Critics' Award as Best Actress the following year for *The Magnificent Ambersons.* She was nominated for *Ambersons* and received three additional nominations, although she never won an Oscar.
   a.   Name the actress.
   b.   Name any one of the films for which she was nominated after *Ambersons.*

19. She played the young Helen Keller on stage, recreated her role in the film, and for a decade remained the youngest person to win an Academy Award.
    a.   Name the actress.
    b.   Name the film.
    c.   In which film version of a Jacqueline Susann novel did she later star?

20. After a distinguished career in the theater, she became a popular character actress in films, specializing in wise old women—sometimes just a bit dotty. Her winning performance was in a 1944 film directed by Clifford Odets and starring Cary Grant as her ne'er-do-well son.
    a.   Name the actress.
    b.   Name the film.
    c.   Name the superior thriller in which she was bedridden and co-starred with Dorothy McGuire, who played a mute girl in danger.

21. She won her award as the indomitable matriarch of a destitute family headed for California to find work during the Depression.
   a.   Name the actress.
   b.   Name the film.

22. One of the busiest and most talented actresses of the forties and fifties won an Oscar as a proper young girl who goes to pieces after her husband and child are killed and is discovered by old friends singing in a Paris saloon.
   a.   Name the actress.
   b.   Name the movie.
   c.   Name the author of the novel upon which the film was based.

23. Name the pictures in which this same actress:
   a.   Was the ingenue in Orson Welles's second film.
   b.   Had been in love with Montgomery Clift before he became a priest, in a Hitchcock film.
   c.   Played the title role of a deceitful actress in one of the screen's great films.

24. As a precocious child as cleverly dishonest as the Bible-selling con man with whom she travels, this actress became the youngest person ever to win an Oscar.
   a.   Name the actress.
   b.   Name the film.
   c.   Name the actor who played the con man.

25. In that most famous of all American films, this actress won for her powerful and stirring performance as the heroine's closest and most loyal servant.
   a.   Name the actress.
   b.   Name the movie.
   c.   What was the name of the character she played?

Answers on page 146.

1951

With the exception of 1939, more excellent American films were released in 1951 than in any other year. This quiz concerns those films.

1. The two films favored to win the Academy Award as Best Picture of 1951 were both highly acclaimed dramas. One was adapted from a novel by Theodore Dreiser, and the other was the screen version of a play by Tennessee Williams.
   a. Name the film adapted from the Dreiser novel.
   b. Name the film adapted by Tennessee Williams from his play.

2. Name the film that won the Best Picture Oscar for 1951.

3. Name the classic, filmed in the Belgian Congo, that won the Best Actor award for one of its stars.

4. One of the strongest dramas of the year was William Wyler's film of Sidney Kingsley's play about the dramatic events that occur on a random day in a New York police station.
   a. Name the film.
   b. Name the leading actor who gave one of his best performances as a man who was fatally uncompromising.
   c. Name the actors who recreated their Broadway roles (along with the nominated Lee Grant) as two inept burglars.

5. For this same film, one of Hollywood's most neglected stars received the second of her three Best Actress nominations.
    a. Name the actress.
    b. Name at least one of the other two films for which she was nominated.

6. The disappointing screen version of a play by Arthur Miller nevertheless won nominations in three acting categories.
    a. Name the film.
    b. Name the nominated performers.
    c. Name the roles the three performers played.

7. Alfred Hitchcock delivered one of his best thrillers, in which psychotic Bruno Anthony attempts to talk tennis star Guy Haines into a double-murder scheme.
    a. Name the film.
    b. Name the actors who played Bruno Anthony and Guy Haines.
    c. Name the actress who played Haines's fiancée, Anne Morton.

8. Leo Genn and Peter Ustinov both received Best Supporting Actor nominations for the year's most expensive film, an MGM spectacle that won a nomination for Best Picture.
    a. Name the film.
    b. Name the two stars of the movie.

9. A sensitive story about a blind veteran won a Best Actor nomination, as well as the New York Film Critics' Award, for its star.
    a. Name the film.
    b. Name the actor.

10. The most decorated American soldier of World War II and a cartoonist who achieved fame during the war were the principals in John Huston's admirable movie about the Civil War.

    a. Name the film.

    b. Name the actor who had been the most-decorated hero.

    c. Name the actor who was the cartoonist.

11. The actor who starred in William Wyler's police drama described earlier gave another vibrant performance as a reporter with a major scoop in a Billy Wilder film.

    a. Name the movie.

    b. Name the other title by which the movie is widely known.

    c. Name the film's leading actress.

12. The stars of 1939's *Destry Rides Again* were reunited in an intriguing movie in which they were both passengers on a plane in trouble.

    a. Name the movie.

    b. Name the reunited stars.

13. Richard Basehart starred in two of the year's most memorable movies, one of which was nominated as Best Picture. The other featured him as a would-be suicide, threatening to jump from a skyscraper.

    a. Name his film that was nominated as Best Picture.

    b. Name the acclaimed German actor who co-starred in that film.

    c. Name the man-on-a-ledge film.

    d. Name the future Oscar winner who made her screen debut in the latter film.

14. Possibly the peak of this singer's short but spectacular career was this MGM musical biography of a legendary opera star.

    a.   Name the movie.

    b.   Name the singer who played the title role.

    c.   Name the film's leading lady.

15. Another MGM film released during this year was the first Technicolor version of the landmark Jerome Kern–Oscar Hammerstein II musical, based on Edna Ferber's novel.

    a.   Name the film.

    b.   Name the performers who played Magnolia, Gaylord, and Julie.

    c.   Name the performers who played these characters in Universal's 1936 version of the musical.

16. Still another MGM musical starred Fred Astaire and Jane Powell; it had a score by Burton Lane and Alan Jay Lerner that included the nominated song, "Too Late Now."
   a. Name the film.
   b. Name the actress, daughter of a great statesman, who made her American screen debut in this film.

17. Joseph L. Mankiewicz's first venture after *All About Eve* was an unusual film about a controversial music-loving doctor.
   a. Name the film.
   b. Name the leading actor.
   c. Name the leading actress.

18. The story of a London urchin who wants to meet Queen Victoria—and does—became a film of considerable charm.
   a. Name the movie.
   b. Name the actress who played Queen Victoria.
   c. Name the actor who played Disraeli.

19. Fred Zinnemann directed a moving film about a war bride's adjustment to life in the United States.
   a. Name the film.
   b. Name the actress who played the war bride.
   c. Name the leading actor.

20. Jane Wyman won a Best Actress nomination for her performance in the first of her fifties tearjerkers.
   a. Name the film.
   b. Name the actress who was a popular star at Warner Brothers during the thirties and who won a Best Supporting Actress nomination for this film.
   c. Name another film of 1951 in which Miss Wyman teamed up with Bing Crosby to sing the year's Oscar-winning song.

Answers on page 148.

BEST SUPPORTING ACTRESS

QUIZ NUMBER TWO

1. In 1938 she received nominations as Best Actress and Best Supporting Actress, winning in the latter category. She and Bette Davis won awards for their performances in the same film, in which she played Aunt Belle Massey.
   a. Name the actress.
   b. Name the film.
   c. Name the picture for which she was nominated as Best Actress and did not win.

2. In Twentieth Century-Fox's answer to MGM's *San Francisco*, this actress scored in the role of Molly O'Leary, the mother of Tyrone Power and Don Ameche and the owner of the cow that started a famous fire.
   a. Name the actress.
   b. Name the picture.
   c. Name a "screwball" comedy in which she played the socialite mother of a dizzy Carole Lombard, who brings home a hobo and turns him into a butler.

3. This appealing dumpling recreated her Broadway role as the scatterbrained sister of a fellow whose best friend was a large, invisible rabbit.
   a. Name the actress.
   b. Name the movie.

101

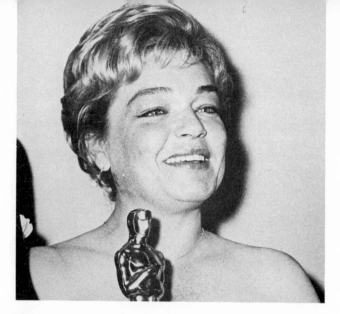

c.   Name an earlier comedy—another role she had created
on the stage—in which she and her sister served several
strangers lethal glasses of elderberry wine.

4. Playing a successful madam who had left her self-righteous husband and their two young sons, this Broadway actress's debut
performance in one of Elia Kazan's best films was impressive
enough to win an Oscar.
a.   Name the actress.
b.   Name the film.
c.   Name the actor who played her husband.

5. As Edie Doyle, a convent-bred young woman, she fell in love
with the man who had betrayed her murdered brother.
a.   Name the actress.
b.   Name the movie.
c.   Name the enjoyable, although quite improbable, Hitchcock entertainment in which she starred opposite Cary
Grant.

6. Re-creating her Broadway role of the mother of a blind young
man determined to live independently, this respected actress
won the Best Supporting Actress award.
a.   Name the actress.
b.   Name the film.
c.   Name the actor who played her blind son.

102

7. As a witty and bright magazine executive, she vainly tried to woo Gregory Peck away from a classy Dorothy McGuire. Her exquisitely judged and moving proposal scene contained perhaps her finest moments in this Oscar-winning performance.
   a. Name the actress.
   b. Name the film.
   c. As Karen Richards, the playwright's wife, she was warm, generous, and gullible in a nominated performance from what film?

8. This was not the first time the Academy had honored her, although it was her first award as a supporting actress. She played a timid, frightened missionary on a star-studded train in an Agatha Christie thriller.
   a. Name the actress.
   b. Name the movie.
   c. Name the actor nominated for his performance (as Best Actor) for playing Christie's famous Belgian sleuth.

9. Torn between her loyalty to her delicate sister and her love for her brutish husband, this actress won her award re-creating her stage role in one of Tennessee Williams's finest plays.
   a. Name the actress.
   b. Name the film.
   c. Name the first in a series of movies in which she did not play a human being.

10. Versatility is a quality this actress has in abundance. In movies and on television she can be funny and beautiful in one role, pathetically moving and drab in another. In the latter type of part, she was an aging, small-town woman who has a brief affair with a local teen-ager, played by Timothy Bottoms.
    a. Name the actress.
    b. Name the film.
    c. Name the Mel Brooks film in which she played the sinister housekeeper, Frau Blucher, an amusing parody of Judith Anderson's Mrs. Danvers.

11. This veteran radio actress enjoyed her greatest movie success as a tough reporter named Sadie Burke, who climbs aboard the bandwagon of a rising demagogic politician.
    a. Name the actress.
    b. Name the movie.
    c. Name the George Stevens epic of modern Texas in which she played the hero's sister.

12. This shy Japanese actress won for her performance in a popular movie starring Marlon Brando in which she and the American soldier she married committed suicide.
    a. Name the actress.
    b. Name the movie.
    c. Name the Rodgers and Hammerstein musical in which she played a Chinese mail-order bride, re-creating her stage role.

13. Famed for her portrayals of Miss Marple, Madame Arcati, and other eccentrics, this treasured comedienne won an Oscar as an addled duchess stranded at an airport in a glittering all-star entertainment from MGM.
  a. Name the actress.
  b. Name the picture.
  c. Name the English film, a faithful adaptation of Wilde's greatest play, in which she played a governess named Miss Prism.

14. Niven, Kerr, Hayworth, and especially Lancaster (with whom she had a special relationship) all stayed at the small English hotel managed by this actress.
  a. Name the actress.
  b. Name this film for which she won.
  c. Name two films, both adapted from famous comedies by Shaw, in which she starred.

15. This Latin actress has been honored on Broadway as well as in Hollywood. She sang, danced, and acted her way to an Oscar in a memorable musical as a Puerto Rican girl named Anita.
  a. Name the actress.
  b. Name the movie.
  c. Name the Rodgers and Hammerstein musical film in which she played an Asian girl, a role Linda Darnell portrayed in an earlier movie.

16. In the screen version of one of the most lacerating plays of our time she was a young college instructor's wife who gets tipsy at an all-night party marked by heavy drinking and painful revelations.
  a. Name the actress.
  b. Name the film.
  c. Name another movie in which she played a new teacher at a difficult New York high school.

17. She won an award as Madame Hortense, an aging woman who desperately wanted to marry Anthony Quinn in a film which became a sort of trademark of that actor.
  a. Name the actress.
  b. Name the film.

18. For her portrait of the hysterical wife of a member of a notorious gang of bank robbers in the thirties, she won an Oscar in her first film role.
- a. Name the actress.
- b. Name the movie.
- c. Name another film for which she was nominated, in which she played a lesbian schoolteacher.

19. Also honored for her first performance in a film was a young actress who became popular as a giggling dumb blonde on a freewheeling television show. She played the girl friend of a dentist whose nurse gets involved in their romance.
- a. Name the actress.
- b. Name the picture.
- c. Name a later film in which she played a girl friend of an amorous Beverly Hills hairdresser.

20. Name the two or more actresses nominated as Best Supporting Actress for each of the following movies:
- a. *Pinky*
- b. *The Last Picture Show*
- c. *All About Eve*
- d. *Gone With the Wind*
- e. *Come to the Stable*
- f. *Tom Jones* (three nominees)

Answers on page 149.

WHAT'S IN A NAME?

Match the real names with the better-known adopted names of the following Academy Award winners.

Quiz Number One

1. Virginia Katherine McMath
2. Thelma Ford
3. Ernest Bickel
4. Rosita Dolores Alverio
5. Lily Chauchoin
6. Frederick Austerlitz
7. Phyllis Isley
8. Shirley Schrift
9. Marion Michael Morrison
10. Patti Woodward
11. Judith Tuvim
12. William Joseph Shields

a. Shelley Winters
b. Fred Astaire
c. Judy Holliday
d. Jane Darwell
e. Barry Fitzgerald
f. Shirley Booth
g. John Wayne
h. Jennifer Jones
i. Fredric March
j. Claudette Colbert
k. Ginger Rogers
l. Rita Moreno

Quiz Number Two

1. Lucille Vanconcells Lang-hanke	a.	Joan Crawford
	b.	Gig Young
2. Janet Cole	c.	Susan Hayward
3. Nathan Birnbaum	d.	Joan Fontaine
4. Edythe Marriner	e.	William Holden
5. Anna Maria Italiano	f.	Kim Hunter
6. Reginald Truscott-Jones	g.	Jane Wyman
7. Leila von Koerber	h.	Marie Dressler
8. Lucille le Sueur	i.	Ray Milland
9. Byron Ellsworth Barr	j.	George Burns
10. Joan de Beauvoir de Havilland	k.	Mary Astor
	l.	Anne Bancroft
11. Sarah Jane Fulks		
12. William Franklin Beedle		

Answers on page 150.

TWO-TIMERS

This quiz concentrates on performers who have won at least two Academy Awards.

1. A British actress won her Oscars playing two of the most famous fictional American characters of our time.
    a. Name the actress.
    b. Name the films.
    c. Name the characters she portrayed.

2. A year after winning her first award, this same actress starred opposite Robert Taylor in a touching love story with a wartime London setting.
    a. Name the movie.
    b. Name an earlier film in which she appeared with Taylor.

3. In his two Academy Award-winning films—one in the thirties, the other in the forties—one of the finest of all American actors played three characters.
    a. Name the actor.
    b. Name the films.

4. The actor just described scored in an extremely broad range of roles. Name the movies in which he played the following:
    a. Robert Browning.

b. A fading movie star who commits suicide by walking into the ocean.
c. Willy Loman.
d. A reporter who falls in love with a supposedly dying Carole Lombard.
e. Samuel L. Clemens.
f. A politician and lawyer clearly patterned after William Jennings Bryan.

5. More closely associated with the stage than with films, this actress's second award came almost forty years after her first. That first Oscar was for Best Actress, the second for Best Supporting Actress.
   a. Name the actress.
   b. Name the two films.
   c. Name the picture based on a Hemingway novel in which she co-starred with Gary Cooper.

6. A young English actress specializing in intense, neurotic characters won her first Oscar for just such a role. Her second award, surprisingly, was for a frothy comedy.
   a. Name the actress.
   b. Name the two films.
   c. Name the leading man in each of the two films.

7. She made the difficult transition from sexpot to character actress, and she has won two supporting awards. In these films she played, respectively, a woman hiding from the Nazis and the selfish mother of a blind girl.
   a. Name the actress.
   b. Name the two films.

8. She won her awards for playing a New York call girl and the blowsy wife of a history professor.
   a. Name the actress.
   b. Name the films.
   c. Name her then-husbands who appeared with her in each of these movies.

9. This same actress co-starred with Montgomery Clift in three pictures.
   a. Name the films.

b. Name the third co-star in each film.

10. A playwright as well as an actor, he has won two Oscars for Best Supporting Actor, the first for a costume epic set in the days when Julius Caesar ruled, and the second concerning an elaborate robbery by a group of international thieves.
    a. Name the actor.
    b. Name the two films.
    c. Name the movie for which he received his first nomination, an expensive MGM spectacle in which he played Nero.

11. As an ex-fighter named Terry Malloy, he referred to himself as a bum who could have been a contender and gave one of his finest performances. It won him an Oscar, as did his later portrayal of the head of a Mafia family.
    a. Name the actor.
    b. Name the two films.
    c. Name the actor who played his smarter brother in the first film.
    d. Name the two actors who won nominations for their performances as his sons in the second film.

12. Name the movies in which the just-described actor:
    a. Played the leader of a motorcycle gang.

b. Made his screen debut as a paraplegic.
c. Played a brute who rapes his sister-in-law.
d. Co-starred with Montgomery Clift.
e. Portrayed an illiterate, idealistic Mexican leader.
f. Fell in love with a Japanese girl.
g. Appeared as Marc Antony.
h. Played a New York gambler in a musical.
i. Portrayed Napoleon.

13. This actress's first Academy Award was earned for playing the mother of an illegitimate child with such warmth and under-statement that she transformed a weepy soap opera into a quite moving film.
   a. Name the actress.
   b. Name the picture.
   c. Name the actor who played both her lover and her son.

14. This same actress later won Best Actress nominations for her portrayals of a woman committed to a mental institution and a wealthy girl deserted by a fortune-hunting suitor.
   a. Name the film for which she won her second Oscar.
   b. Name the other film.

15. In her early Warner Brothers days the foregoing actress was often cast opposite a dashing matinee idol. Name the actor and at least three of the films in which they appeared together.

16. Her first of two Best Actress awards was for a film in which she was gradually being driven insane by her husband. Her second was for portraying a woman who insisted she was the sole survivor of the Czar's immediate family, which had been murdered during the Russian revolution.
   a. Name the actress.
   b. Name the two films.
   c. Name the actor who played her scheming husband in the first film.

17. Name a film in which this same actress co-starred with:
   a. Humphrey Bogart
   b. Cary Grant
   c. Gregory Peck

18. In his diffident, modest manner he was the epitome of the strong, silent, upstanding American. His two awards were for his portrayals of brave, simple men: an authentic hero of World War I and a Western sheriff willing to stand alone against a trio of vengeful outlaws.
   a. Name the actor.
   b. Name the two films.
   c. Name at least one of two films in which he co-starred with the actress in the two preceding questions.

19. This actor had been playing character roles for many years. Then, within a five-year period, he won two Best Supporting Actor awards and went on to become a major star. His awards were for his performances as the fiery brother of a revolutionary Mexican leader and as the painter Paul Gauguin.
   a. Name the actor.
   b. Name the two films.
   c. Name the stars who played his brother in the first film and a fellow artist in the second.

20. For portraying Anna Held and a Chinese peasant named O-lan, this fragile actress won two Academy Awards for Best Actress in an astonishingly brief film career. Name her.

21. Name the only performer who won an Academy Award for a supporting role and later won an Oscar for a leading role.

22. Since the early fifties, the foregoing actor has often played harassed, ambitious urban Americans. An expert farceur, he won his Best Actor award for a dramatic role, an outwardly successful but desperately confused businessman.

  a. Name the film.
  b. Name the actor who played his business associate and received a Best Supporting Actor nomination.

23. The actor described in the two preceding questions won the Best Supporting Actor award for his performance as an inventive albeit inept ensign in the movie version of a famous Broadway play.

  a. Name the film.
  b. Name the actor who played the title role.
  c. Name the actor who played the captain of the ensign's ship.

24. Name the following films, for which he was nominated in the Best Actor category, in which this same actor:

  a. Played an alcoholic.
  b. Appeared in drag.
  c. Was in possession of a key that was important to many of his company's executives.

25. Two of the twice-winning actresses have appeared as twin sisters.

  a. Name the actress who has done this twice and the titles of the films.
  b. Name the actress for whom once was enough and the title of her film.

Answers on page 151.

GENERAL QUIZ
NUMBER TWO

1. Only three people have been nominated for acting and writing awards for a single film.
    a. Name the people and the films for which they were nominated.
    b. Which, if any, won in either or both categories?

2. In 1973 Marvin Hamlisch won three Academy Awards: for Best Musical Score, Best Song, and Best Musical Adaptation. Name the films for which he won.

3. Although James Dean became and remains a legend, he starred in only three films.
    a. Name the films.
    b. Name the film(s) for which he was nominated as Best Actor.

4. Oscar-wise, what do Kirk Douglas, Henry Fonda, Judy Garland, Walter Huston, and Ryan O'Neal have in common?

5. Barbara Stanwyck received four Best Actress nominations. Name the films in which she portrayed the following:
    a. A self-sacrificing mother.
    b. An amoral blond murderess.
    c. An entertainer named Sugarpuss O'Shea.
    d. A bedridden neurotic.

6. Oscar-wise, what do Bette Davis, Olivia de Havilland, Greer Garson, Audrey Hepburn, Charlton Heston, Fredric March, and Barbra Streisand have in common?

7. In 1935 four actors were nominated for the Best Actor award, and no less than three were nominees for the same film.
    a. Name the film for which these three were nominated.
    b. Name the three actors.
    c. Name the actor who won the award.

8. Several films have claimed Academy Award nominations in all four acting categories. Name the nominees from the following movies:
    a. *A Streetcar Named Desire*
    b. *Johnny Belinda*
    c. *My Man Godfrey*
    d. *Sunset Boulevard*
    e. *Network*
    f. *Bonnie and Clyde*
    g. *From Here to Eternity*
    h. *Who's Afraid of Virginia Woolf?*
    i. *Mrs. Miniver*
    j. *For Whom the Bell Tolls*
    k. *Guess Who's Coming to Dinner*

9. In addition to *Network, Bonnie and Clyde, From Here to Eternity,* and *Mrs. Miniver,* four other films received five acting nominations. Name the nominees for:
    a. *All About Eve*
    b. *On the Waterfront*
    c. *Tom Jones*
    d. *The Godfather Part II*

10. In 1943 she won the New York Film Critics' Award as Best Actress for her portrayal of the ambitious and possessive sister of Joan Leslie. The Academy did not nominate her for her performance—and, indeed, it never has.
    a. Name the actress.
    b. Name the picture.

11. Montgomery Clift received four nominations, including one for Best Supporting Actor. Name the films he was nominated for

in which he played the following:
   a. A soldier stationed in Hawaii.
   b. A soldier stationed in postwar Europe.
   c. A victim of Nazi persecution.
   d. An ambitious poor relation.

12. In 1941 and 1966 sisters were in competition for the Best Actress Oscar.
   a. Name the two sets of sisters.
   b. Name the films for which each was nominated.

13. Al Pacino won nominations in four consecutive years.
   a. Name the movies for which he was nominated.
   b. Name the men—two in all—who directed those four films.

14. Oscar-wise, what do Van Heflin, Claire Trevor, Ray Milland, James Dunn, Anne Baxter, and Thomas Mitchell have in common?

15. One actress who has never won an Academy Award has more Best Actress nominations than any other nonwinner.
   a. Name the actress.
   b. Name at least three of the films for which she has been nominated.

16. Oscar-wise, what do Supporting Actress and Actor winners Fay Bainter, Walter Brennan, Hugh Griffith, Burl Ives, Harold Russell, and Teresa Wright have in common?

17. Three actors have been nominated posthumously for Best Actor.
   a. Name them.
   b. Which actor(s), if any, won?

18. The screen's most elegant and accomplished light comedian, Cary Grant, received two Oscar nominations, neither of which was for a comedy. Name the two films.

19. Among Henry Fonda's roles are Abraham Lincoln, Mister Roberts, Frank James, Tom Joad, and Admiral Nimitz. Name each of the roles and films for which he has been nominated.

20. Rosalind Russell received four Best Actress nominations. Name those films in which she portrayed the following:
   a.   An aspiring writer from Ohio, living in Greenwich Village.
   b.   A tragic O'Neill heroine.
   c.   A famous nurse.
   d.   A madcap socialite who becomes the unlikely guardian of her young nephew.

21. Miss Russell unforgettably played, in perhaps the fastest-paced comedy ever made, a role previously played on film by Pat O'Brien and later by Jack Lemmon.
   a.   Name the title of this film.
   b.   Name the title of the play on which it was based (which is also the title of the other film versions).
   c.   Name her co-star.
   d.   Name the director of this classic.

22. Nineteen forty-seven was a peak year for this sensitive actor who was typed as "Depression's child," a poor guy who needed a break. His portrayal of a corrupted boxer won him a Best Actor nomination.
   a.   Name the actor.
   b.   Name the movie.
   c.   Name that year's Oscar-winning film about religious prejudice in which he co-starred.
   d.   Name his debut film, for which he received a nomination for Best Supporting Actor, for playing a bitter young composer.

23. Name the choreographers who were presented with honorary Oscars in:
   a.   1951
   b.   1961
   c.   1968

24. Name at least three Academy Award winners who appeared in *The Poseidon Adventure*.

25. A special award for outstanding achievement by a juvenile performer has been given in the years listed below. Match the years with the performers.

a.	1934	1.	Bobby Driscoll
b.	1938 (two awards)	2.	Deanna Durbin
c.	1939	3.	Peggy Ann Garner
d.	1944	4.	Judy Garland
e.	1945	5.	Ivan Jandl
f.	1946	6.	Claude Jarman, Jr.
g.	1948	7.	Hayley Mills
h.	1949	8.	Margaret O'Brien
i.	1954 (two awards)	9.	Mickey Rooney
j.	1960	10.	Shirley Temple
		11.	Jon Whiteley
		12.	Vincent Winter

Answers on page 153.

119

TRUE OR FALSE

1. Seven of the first eleven Best Director Awards went to men whose given name was Frank.

2. Dame Judith Anderson's only Oscar was won for her portrayal of Mrs. Danvers in *Rebecca*.

3. Anthony Perkins made his movie debut in *Friendly Persuasion* and was nominated as Best Supporting Actor.

4. Celeste Holm acted for Joseph L. Mankiewicz in both *A Letter to Three Wives* and *All About Eve* but appeared in only one of those films.

5. Three of Susan Hayward's five Best Actress nominations were for portraying alcoholics.

6. One of the films for which Elia Kazan won an Oscar was *A Streetcar Named Desire*.

7. Lionel Barrymore created the role of Andy Hardy's father in MGM's popular series.

8. One of the screen's great comediennes, Jean Arthur, was never nominated for an Academy Award.

9. For *The Godfather Part II* Francis Ford Coppola and his father, Carmine, both won Oscars.

10. Rosalind Russell's clowning as that supergossip, Sylvia Fowler, in *The Women* was the first of her several nominations.

11. Gene Kelly's only nomination as an actor was for *An American in Paris*.

12. Bette Davis and Katharine Hepburn both portrayed characters named Jane Hudson.

13. Two of Elizabeth Taylor's nominations were for *A Place in the Sun* and *Who's Afraid of Virginia Woolf?*

14. Katharine Hepburn and Bob Hope once co-starred in a comedy.

15. Never the cowboy type, Humphrey Bogart was cast by Warner Brothers only in contemporary action, adventure, crime, or war movies.

16. Edward G. Robinson was never nominated for an Oscar.

17. Joan Blondell's only nomination was for her performance as Aunt Sissy in *A Tree Grows in Brooklyn*.

18. Katharine Hepburn and Spencer Tracy, respectively, received more nominations than any other actress or actor.

19. George C. Scott is the only person who refused to accept his Oscar.

20. Ingrid Bergman is the only two-time winner of the Best Actress award who later received a Best Supporting Actress award.

Answers on page 155.

ANSWERS TO THE QUIZZES

General Quiz Number One
1. Only one of these fifteen actors is an Oscar winner: Ginger Rogers for *Kitty Foyle*.
2. a. Julie
   b. Lionel
   c. Alice
   d. Charles
   e. Melvyn
   f. José
   g. Barry
   h. Jane
   i. Hugh
   j. Susan
   k. Josephine
   l. Kim
   m. Glenda
   n. Ben
   o. Shirley
   p. Grace
   q. George
   r. Thomas
   s. Tatum
   t. Donna
   u. Maximilian
   v. George C.
   w. Maggie
   x. John
   y. Gig

Best Actor Quiz Number One
1. Wallace Beery for *The Champ* and Fredric March for *Dr. Jekyll and Mr. Hyde*
2. Spencer Tracy for *Captains Courageous* (1937) and *Boys Town* (1938)
3. a. *The Philadelphia Story*
   b. *Mr. Smith Goes to Washington*

4. a. *It's a Wonderful Life*
   b. *Harvey*
   c. *Anatomy of a Murder*
5. a. Paul Muni
   b. *The Story of Louis Pasteur*
   c. *Juarez*
6. a. *I Am a Fugitive from a Chain Gang*
   b. *Scarface*
7. a. *The Valiant*
   b. *The Life of Emile Zola*
   c. *The Last Angry Man*
8. a. Sidney Poitier
   b. *Lilies of the Field*
   c. *Guess Who's Coming to Dinner*
9. a. *The Defiant Ones*
   b. Tony Curtis
   c. Theodore Bikel
10. a. Maximilian Schell
   b. *Judgment at Nuremberg*
   c. Spencer Tracy, Burt Lancaster,
      Richard Widmark, and Marlene Dietrich
11. a. Alec Guinness
   b. *The Bridge on the River Kwai*
   c. William Holden
   d. Sessue Hayakawa
12. a. Paul Scofield
   b. *A Man for All Seasons*
   c. Wendy Hiller and Susannah York
13. a. Art Carney
   b. *Harry and Tonto*
   c. *The Late Show*
14. a. Emil Jannings
   b. *The Blue Angel*
   c. Marlene Dietrich
15. a. Warner Baxter
   b. *42nd Street*
   c. Ruby Keeler
   d. The *Crime Doctor* series,
      in which he played Dr. Ordway

16. a. Charlton Heston
    b. *Ben-Hur*
    c. *The Ten Commandments*
    d. *Planet of the Apes*
17. a. Lionel Barrymore
    b. *A Free Soul*
    c. Dr. Gillespie
    d. *Rasputin and the Empress*

18. a. *You Can't Take It With You*
    b. *It's a Wonderful Life*
    c. *Dinner at Eight*
19. a. David Niven
    b. *Separate Tables*
    c. Deborah Kerr
20. a. Rod Steiger
    b. *In the Heat of the Night*
    c. *The Pawnbroker*

Best Picture
1. *Wings*
2. *The Godfather*
3. *The Life of Émile Zola*
4. b. William Dieterle
5. *The Broadway Melody*
6. *The Greatest Show on Earth*
7. Cecil B. De Mille
8. a. *Grand Hotel*
   b. Greta Garbo, John Barrymore, Joan Crawford, Wallace Beery, Lionel Barrymore, Lewis Stone, and Jean Hersholt
   c. *Weekend at the Waldorf*
9. a. *Hamlet*
   b. Laurence Olivier
   c. *Henry V* and *Richard III*
10. a. James Cagney, Dick Powell, Joe E. Brown, Olivia de Havilland, Mickey Rooney, Hugh Herbert, Ian Hunter, Frank McHugh, Anita Louise, and Arthur Treacher
    b. Marlon Brando, James Mason, John Gielgud, Louis Calhern, Edmond O'Brien, Greer Garson, and Deborah Kerr
    c. Leslie Howard and Norma Shearer; Laurence Harvey and Susan Shentall; Leonard Whiting and Olivia Hussey
11. *In the Heat of the Night*
12. a. *An American in Paris*
    b. Leslie Caron
    c. Arthur Freed (producer) and Vincente Minnelli (director)

13. a. *Mutiny on the Bounty*
  b. Clark Gable and Charles Laughton
  c. Marlon Brando and Trevor Howard
14. *Cimarron*
15. a. *Rebecca*
  b. Alfred Hitchcock
  c. No one; the character did not appear in the film.
16. a. *Spellbound*
  b. *The Paradine Case*
17. *All the King's Men*
18. c. Robert Rossen
19. a. *The Great Ziegfeld*
  b. William Powell and Myrna Loy
  c. Florenz Ziegfeld and Billie Burke
20. a. *Around the World in 80 Days*
  b. David Niven
  c. Cantinflas

Best Actor Quiz Number Two
  1. a. George Arliss
    b. *Disraeli*
    c. Bette Davis
  2. a. Gene Hackman
    b. *The French Connection*
    c. *Bonnie and Clyde*
  3. a. Clark Gable
    b. *It Happened One Night*
    c. Carole Lombard
  4. a. Charles Laughton
    b. *The Private Life of Henry VIII*
    c. Elsa Lanchester
  5. a. *The Barretts of Wimpole Street*
    b. *Witness for the Prosecution*
    c. *Les Misérables*
    d. *Advise and Consent*
  6. a. Bing Crosby
    b. *Going My Way*
    c. *The Country Girl*

7. a. Bob Hope and Dorothy Lamour
   b. Singapore, Zanzibar, Morocco, Utopia (Alaska), Rio, Bali, and Hong Kong
8. a. José Ferrer
   b. *Cyrano de Bergerac*
   c. *Moulin Rouge*
9. a. Ray Milland
   b. *The Lost Weekend*
   c. *Beau Geste*
10. a. William Holden
    b. *Sunset Boulevard*
    c. *Stalag 17*
    d. *Stalag 17*
11. a. *Our Town*
    b. *Picnic*
    c. *Network*
    d. *The Country Girl*
12. a. Burt Lancaster
    b. *Elmer Gantry*
13. a. *From Here to Eternity*
    b. *Judgment at Nuremberg*
    c. *Seven Days in May*
    d. *Bird Man of Alcatraz*
14. Gregory Peck for *To Kill a Mockingbird*
15. a. *The Keys of the Kingdom*
    b. *The Yearling*
    c. *Gentleman's Agreement*
    d. *Twelve O'Clock High*
16. a. *Roman Holiday*
    b. *Moby Dick*
    c. *Duel in the Sun*
    d. *On the Beach*
17. a. Lee Marvin
    b. *Cat Ballou*
    c. *Paint Your Wagon*
18. Jack Nicholson for *One Flew Over the Cuckoo's Nest*
19. a. *Five Easy Pieces*
    b. *The Last Detail*   c. *Chinatown*
20. *Easy Rider*

Best Director
1. Frank Borzage
2. Frank Lloyd
3. a. Norman Taurog
   b. *Skippy*
4. a. John Ford
   b. *The Informer*
   c. *The Grapes of Wrath*
   d. *The Quiet Man*
5. a. Frank Capra
   b. *Mr. Deeds Goes to Town*
   c. Jean Arthur
6. a. Leo McCarey
   b. *The Awful Truth*
7. *Make Way for Tomorrow*
8. a. John Huston
   b. *The Treasure of the Sierra Madre*
9. a. *Key Largo*
   b. Humphrey Bogart
   c. Claire Trevor
10. a. Joseph L. Mankiewicz
    b. *A Letter to Three Wives*
    c. Jeanne Crain, Linda Darnell, and Ann Sothern
11. a. *The Barefoot Contessa*
    b. *Julius Caesar*
    c. *Guys and Dolls*
    d. *Suddenly, Last Summer*
    e. *Cleopatra*
12. a. Bob Fosse
    b. *Cabaret*
13. a. *Sweet Charity*
    b. Gwen Verdon
    c. *The Nights of Cabiria*
14. a. *Lenny*
    b. Dustin Hoffman
    c. Valerie Perrine
15. a. George Stevens
    b. *A Place in the Sun*
    c. Montgomery Clift, Elizabeth Taylor, and Shelley Winters

16. a. *Giant*
   b. Rock Hudson
   c. Elizabeth Taylor
   d. James Dean
17. a. *Shane*
   b. Alan Ladd
   c. Van Heflin and Jean Arthur
   d. Brandon de Wilde
18. a. *Woman of the Year*
   b. *Alice Adams*
   c. *I Remember Mama*
   d. *The Diary of Anne Frank*
19. a. Mike Nichols
   b. *The Graduate*
   c. Dustin Hoffman, Anne Bancroft, and Katharine Ross
20. a. *Catch-22*
   b. *Who's Afraid of Virginia Woolf?*
   c. *Carnal Knowledge*

Best Actor Quiz Number Three
   1. a. Rex Harrison
      b. *My Fair Lady*
      c. *Cleopatra*
   2. a. *Anna and the King of Siam*
      b. *The King and I*
   3. a. James Cagney
      b. *Yankee Doodle Dandy*
      c. George M. Cohan
   4. *The Public Enemy* and *Love Me or Leave Me*
   5. a. Ronald Colman
      b. *A Double Life*
      c. Shelley Winters
   6. a. *Bulldog Drummond* and *Condemned*
      b. *Random Harvest*
   7. a. *Lost Horizon*
      b. *A Tale of Two Cities*
      c. *The Light That Failed*

8. a. John Wayne
   b. *True Grit*
   c. *Sands of Iwo Jima*
9. a. *The Quiet Man*
   b. *Stagecoach*
   c. *The Long Voyage Home*
10. a. George C. Scott
    b. *Patton*
    c. Karl Malden
11. a. *Anatomy of a Murder*
       and *The Hustler*
    b. *The Hustler*
12. a. Broderick Crawford
    b. *All the King's Men*
    c. *Born Yesterday*
13. a. Cliff Robertson
    b. *Charly*
    c. Claire Bloom
14. a. Laurence Olivier
    b. *Hamlet*
    c. *Henry V, Richard III,*
       and *Othello*

15. a. *Wuthering Heights*
    b. *Rebecca*
    c. *Pride and Prejudice*
    d. *Carrie*
16. a. Peter Finch
    b. *Network*
    c. *Sunday Bloody Sunday*
17. a. Humphrey Bogart
    b. *The African Queen*
    c. Robert Morley
18. a. Victor McLaglen
    b. *The Informer*
    c. *The Quiet Man*
19. a. Ernest Borgnine
    b. *Marty*
    c. *From Here to Eternity*
20. a. Yul Brynner
    b. *The King and I*
    c. *Anastasia*

Humphrey Bogart
1. *The Maltese Falcon* and *High Sierra*
2. a. *Across the Pacific*
   b. Mary Astor and Sydney Greenstreet
3. a. *The Caine Mutiny*
   b. José Ferrer, Van Johnson, and Fred MacMurray
4. *Casablanca*
5. *Passage to Marseilles*
6. *To Have and Have Not*
7. *The Big Sleep*
8. *Dark Passage*
9. *Key Largo*
10. *The Treasure of the Sierra Madre*
11. *Beat the Devil*

12. *The Petrified Forest*
13. *The Desperate Hours*
14. *We're No Angels*
15. a. *The African Queen*
    b. *The Maltese Falcon, Across the Pacific, The Treasure of the Sierra Madre, Key Largo,* and *Beat the Devil*
16. *Sabrina*
17. a. *Dead End*
    b. Marjorie Main
    c. Billy Halop, Leo Gorcey, Huntz Hall, Bobby Jordan, Gabriel Dell, and Bernard Punsley
18. *Dark Victory*
19. *The Two Mrs. Carrolls* with Barbara Stanwyck and *Conflict* with Alexis Smith
20. a. *The Maltese Falcon*
    b. *The Petrified Forest*
    c. *The Big Sleep*
    d. *The Caine Mutiny*
    e. *The Treasure of the Sierra Madre*
    f. *The African Queen*

Best Picture and Director Quiz Number One
1. a. John Ford
   b. *How Green Was My Valley*
2. a. *Marty*
   b. Rod Steiger
3. c. Delbert Mann
4. a. *All About Eve*
   b. Bette Davis, Anne Baxter, George Sanders, Celeste Holm, and Thelma Ritter
   c. Marilyn Monroe
5. Joseph L. Mankiewicz
6. a. *It Happened One Night* and *One Flew Over the Cuckoo's Nest*
   b. Frank Capra and Milos Forman
7. a. *You Can't Take It With You*
   b. Jean Arthur
   c. James Stewart

8. a. *Mr. Deeds Goes to Town, Mr. Smith Goes to Washington,* and *Meet John Doe*

 b. James Stewart played Jefferson Smith, and Gary Cooper played the other two characters.

 c. *It's a Wonderful Life*

9. a. *Gentleman's Agreement*

 b. Elia Kazan

 c. Gregory Peck and Dorothy McGuire

 d. Dean Stockwell

10. *On the Waterfront*

11. a. *A Streetcar Named Desire*

 b. *A Streetcar Named Desire, Viva Zapata!,* and *On the Waterfront*

 c. James Dunn, Celeste Holm, Anthony Quinn, Eva Marie Saint, and Jo Van Fleet

12. a. *Rocky*

 b. John G. Avildsen

 c. *Save the Tiger*

13. a. George Cukor

 b. *My Fair Lady*

14. a. Ingrid Bergman

 b. Ronald Colman

 c. Judy Holliday

 d. James Stewart

 e. Rex Harrison

15. a. William Wyler

 b. *Mrs. Miniver* and *The Best Years of Our Lives*

16. *Ben-Hur*

17. John Ford won for *The Grapes of Wrath* (1940) and *How Green Was My Valley* (1941). Joseph L. Mankiewicz won for *A Letter to Three Wives* (1949) and *All About Eve* (1950).

18. a. Lewis Milestone

 b. *All Quiet on the Western Front*

 c. Lew Ayres

19. a. Jerome Robbins

 b. Robert Wise

 c. *West Side Story*

20. *The Sound of Music*

Katharine Hepburn

1. *Woman of the Year*
2. *Bringing Up Baby*
3. *Holiday*
4. *Little Women*
5. *Long Day's Journey into Night*
6. *Adam's Rib*
7. *The Rainmaker*
8. *The African Queen*
9. *Summertime*
10. *Pat and Mike*
11. *Stage Door*
12. *Keeper of the Flame*
13. *A Bill of Divorcement*
14. *The Philadelphia Story*
15. *Stage Door Canteen*
16. *State of the Union*
17. *The Trojan Women*
18. *Suddenly, Last Summer*
19. *Dragon Seed*
20. *Mary of Scotland*

Best Picture and Director Quiz Number Two

1. a. Francis Ford Coppola
   b. *The Godfather* and *The Godfather Part II*
   c. *The Godfather Part II*
2. a. Tony Richardson
   b. *Tom Jones*
   c. *Look Back in Anger*
3. a. David Lean
   b. *The Bridge on the River Kwai* and *Lawrence of Arabia*
   c. Alec Guinness (Jack Hawkins also appeared in both films)
   d. *Great Expectations* and *Oliver Twist*
4. a. *The French Connection*
   b. William Friedkin
   c. *The Exorcist*
5. a. *Gigi*
   b. Vincente Minnelli
   c. None were nominated, although Maurice Chevalier received a special Oscar for his half century of contributions to the entertainment industry.
6. a. *Casablanca*
   b. Michael Curtiz
   c. Claude Rains played Renault, Conrad Veidt played Strasser, and Sydney Greenstreet played Ferrari.
   d. Dooley Wilson
7. a. *Midnight Cowboy*

b. John Schlesinger
c. Jon Voight
8. a. Frank Lloyd
b. *Cavalcade*
9. a. *From Here to Eternity*
b. Fred Zinnemann
c. Burt Lancaster, Montgomery Clift, and Deborah Kerr
10. a. *A Man for All Seasons*
b. Sir Thomas More
c. Henry VIII
11. a. *High Noon*
b. *Oklahoma!*
c. *The Search*
d. *The Nun's Story*
12. a. *The Sting*
b. George Roy Hill
c. Robert Shaw
13. a. *Going My Way*
b. Leo McCarey
14. a. *Patton*
b. Franklin J. Schaffner
15. a. *Oliver!*
b. Carol Reed
c. Mark Lester
16. a. *The Third Man*
b. *The Fallen Idol*
c. *Odd Man Out*
17. a. *The Lost Weekend*
b. Billy Wilder
18. a. *The Apartment*
b. Jack Lemmon and Shirley MacLaine
c. Fred MacMurray
19. a. *Sunset Boulevard*
b. *Some Like It Hot*
c. *Double Indemnity*
d. *Sabrina*
20. a. *Gone With the Wind*
b. Victor Fleming
c. George Cukor and Sam Wood

Best Actress Quiz Number One
1. Katharine Hepburn for *The Lion in Winter* and Barbra Streisand for *Funny Girl*
2. Katharine Hepburn for *Morning Glory, Guess Who's Coming to Dinner*, and *The Lion in Winter*
3. Luise Rainer for *The Great Ziegfeld* and *The Good Earth*
4. a. Audrey Hepburn
   b. Shirley Booth
   c. Barbra Streisand
   d. Jennifer Jones
   e. Louise Fletcher
5. Judy Holliday for *Born Yesterday*
6. a. *Dangerous* (Davis) and *Suspicion* (Fontaine)
   b. *Of Human Bondage* (for which Davis was not even nominated) and *Rebecca* (Fontaine)
7. Luise Rainer (for *The Great Ziegfeld* in 1936 and *The Good Earth* in 1937) and Davis (for *Jezebel* in 1938)
8. a. *Mildred Pierce*
   b. *Letty Lynton, Sadie McKee, The Last of Mrs. Cheyney, Susan and God, Daisy Kenyon, Harriet Craig,* and *Queen Bee;* also, although more indirectly, *Dancing Lady, The Gorgeous Hussy, The Bride Wore Red, Mannequin, A Woman's Face, They All Kissed the Bride, This Woman Is Dangerous,* and *Female on the Beach*
9. a. *The Song of Bernadette*
   b. *Cluny Brown, Portrait of Jennie; Madame Bovary; Carrie; Ruby Gentry; Good Morning, Miss Dove;* and (more indirectly) *Indiscretion of an American Wife*
10. a. *Since You Went Away*
    b. *Duel in the Sun*
    c. *Love Letters*
    d. *Love Is a Many-Splendored Thing*
11. a. *The Country Girl*
    b. *Mogambo*
12. a. *Dial M for Murder, Rear Window,* and *To Catch a Thief*
    b. Ray Milland in *Dial M for Murder* (Robert Cummings co-starred), James Stewart in *Rear Window*, and Cary Grant in *To Catch a Thief*
13. a. *Network*

   b. *Bonnie and Clyde* or *Chinatown*

14. a. Jane Fonda

   b. *Klute*

   c. Donald Sutherland

15. *They Shoot Horses, Don't They?*

16. a. *I'll Cry Tomorrow* (Roth), *With a Song in My Heart* (Froman), *I Want to Live!* (Graham)

   b. *I Want to Live!*

   c. *Smash-Up—The Story of a Woman* and *My Foolish Heart.*

17. a. Loretta Young

   b. *The Farmer's Daughter*

   c. Joseph Cotten

18. a. Sophia Loren

   b. *Two Women*

19. a. Anna Magnani

   b. *The Rose Tattoo*

   c. *The Fugitive Kind* (adapted from Williams's play *Orpheus Descending*)

   d. Maureen Stapleton

20. a. Jane Wyman

   b. *Johnny Belinda*

   c. *The Lost Weekend* and *The Yearling*

1939

  1. Vivien Leigh, Olivia de Havilland, and Hattie McDaniel

  2. a. Butterfly McQueen

   b. Ona Munson

   c. Laura Hope Crews

   d. Harry Davenport

   e. Evelyn Keyes and Ann Rutherford

  3. a. *Wuthering Heights*

   b. Merle Oberon, Laurence Olivier, David Niven, Geraldine Fitzgerald, Donald Crisp, Flora Robson, Hugh Williams, Cecil Kellaway, Leo G. Carroll, and Miles Mander

  4. a. Robert Donat

   b. *Goodbye, Mr. Chips*

  5. a. *Mr. Smith Goes to Washington* and *Only Angels Have Wings*

   b. *The Hunchback of Notre Dame*

    c. *Stagecoach*

6. a. Frank Morgan
    b. Ray Bolger
    c. Jack Haley
    d. Bert Lahr
    e. Margaret Hamilton
    f. Billie Burke
    g. Clara Blandick

7. Claude Rains, Edward Arnold, Guy Kibbee, Thomas Mitchell, Eugene Pallette, Beulah Bondi, H. B. Warner, Harry Carey, Ruth Donnelly, Grant Mitchell, Porter Hall, and William Demarest

8. a. Edna May Oliver
    b. *Drums Along the Mohawk*
    c. *The Story of Vernon and Irene Castle*
    d. Aunt March in *Little Women* and Aunt Betsey in *David Copperfield*

9. John Wayne, Claire Trevor, Thomas Mitchell, George Bancroft, Andy Devine, John Carradine, Louise Platt, Donald Meek, Berton Churchill, Tim Holt, and Chris-Pin Martin

10. *The Story of Alexander Graham Bell*

11. Norma Shearer, Joan Crawford, Rosalind Russell, Mary Boland, Paulette Goddard, Joan Fontaine, Lucile Watson, Phyllis Povah, Florence Nash, Virginia Weidler, Ruth Hussey, Margaret Dumont, and Marjorie Main

12. a. *Intermezzo: A Love Story*
    b. Leslie Howard

13. a. *Gunga Din*
    b. Sam Jaffe

14. a. *Destry Rides Again*
    b. "See What the Boys in the Back Room Will Have"

15. a. *The Private Lives of Elizabeth and Essex*
    b. *The Old Maid*
    c. *Dark Victory*

16. a. *Ninotchka*
    b. Ina Claire
    c. *Two-Faced Woman*

17. a. Mickey Rooney
    b. *Babes in Arms*
    c. Andy Hardy

  d. Lewis Stone was Judge Hardy (although he did not create the role), Fay Holden was Mrs. Hardy, and Cecilia Parker was Marian.

18. *Wuthering Heights*
19. a. *Love Affair*
  b. Maria Ouspenskaya
  c. *Cimarron, Theodora Goes Wild, The Awful Truth,* and *I Remember Mama*
20. a. *Idiot's Delight*
  b. *Of Mice and Men*
  c. *Made for Each Other*
  d. *Jesse James*
  e. *Confessions of a Nazi Spy*
  f. *The Rains Came*
  g. *Young Mr. Lincoln*
  h. *The Cat and the Canary*
  i. *Golden Boy*
  j. *Stanley and Livingstone*

Best Actress Quiz Number Two
 1. a. Claudette Colbert
  b. *It Happened One Night*
  c. *Since You Went Away*
 2. a. Joanne Woodward
  b. *The Three Faces of Eve*
  c. *Rachel, Rachel*
 3. a. Greer Garson
  b. *Mrs. Miniver*
  c. Walter Pidgeon
 4. a. *Blossoms in the Dust, Madame Curie, Mrs. Parkington,* and *The Valley of Decision*
  b. *Goodbye, Mr. Chips*
  c. *Sunrise at Campobello*
 5. a. Patricia Neal
  b. *Hud*
  c. Paul Newman
 6. a. Ellen Burstyn
  b. *Alice Doesn't Live Here Anymore*
  c. Kris Kristofferson

7. a. *The Exorcist*
    b. Linda Blair
    c. Max von Sydow
8. a. Julie Christie
    b. *Darling*
    c. *Doctor Zhivago*
9. a. Maggie Smith
    b. *The Prime of Miss Jean Brodie*
    c. *Othello*
10. a. Liza Minnelli
    b. *Cabaret*
    c. Michael York
11. a. Janet Gaynor
    b. *A Star Is Born*
    c. *The Young in Heart*
12. a. Mary Pickford
    b. *Coquette*
13. a. Norma Shearer
    b. *The Divorcee*
    c. Irving Thalberg
14. a. *Private Lives*
    b. *Idiot's Delight*
    c. *The Women*
    d. *Romeo and Juliet*
15. a. Anne Bancroft
    b. *The Miracle Worker*
    c. *The Graduate*
16. a. Marie Dressler
    b. *Min and Bill*
    c. *Dinner at Eight*
17. a. Julie Andrews
    b. *Mary Poppins*
    c. Eliza Doolittle in *My Fair Lady*
18. a. *The Sound of Music*
    b. Christopher Plummer
    c. *Thoroughly Modern Millie*
19. a. Simone Signoret
    b. *Room at the Top*
    c. Laurence Harvey
20. *Ship of Fools*

Best Song

	1.		2.		3.	
a.	8	a.	4	a.	14
b.	6	b.	9	b.	2
c.	15	c.	5	c.	5
d.	10	d.	7	d.	7
e.	12	e.	10	e.	8
f.	14	f.	8	f.	9
g.	9	g.	1	g.	11
h.	11	h.	6	h.	12
i.	13	i.	2	i.	13
j.	5	j.	3	j.	4
k.	3			k.	15
l.	2			l.	6
m.	4			m.	3
n.	7			n.	10
o.	1			o.	1

Best Supporting Actor Quiz Number One
1. *Come and Get It, Kentucky,* and *The Westerner*
2. a. Barry Fitzgerald
   b. *Going My Way*
   c. Bing Crosby
3. a. Harold Russell
   b. *The Best Years of Our Lives*
4. a. John Houseman
   b. *The Paper Chase*
   c. Timothy Bottoms
5. a. Jason Robards
   b. *All the President's Men*
   c. Robert Redford
6. Edmund Gwenn in *Miracle on 34th Street*
7. a. *Foreign Correspondent*
   b. *Pride and Prejudice*
   c. *Mister 880*
8. a. Lee J. Cobb, Karl Malden, and Rod Steiger
   b. Robert De Niro, Michael V. Gazzo, and Lee Strasberg
   c. Robert De Niro
9. a. Melvyn Douglas
   b. *Hud*

    c. *Ninotchka*
10. a. George Sanders
    b. *All About Eve*
    c. Addison De Witt was the character based on George Jean Nathan.
11. a. Joseph Schildkraut
    b. *The Life of Émile Zola*
    c. Gale Sondergaard
12. a. Sydney Greenstreet
    b. *The Maltese Falcon*
    c. Peter Lorre
13. a. John Mills
    b. *Ryan's Daughter*
    c. Hayley Mills
14. a. Claude Rains
    b. *Mr. Smith Goes to Washington, Casablanca, Mr. Skeffington,* and *Notorious*
15. *Now, Voyager* and *Deception*
16. a. George Kennedy
    b. *Cool Hand Luke*
17. a. Joel Grey
    b. *Cabaret*
18. a. Burl Ives
    b. *The Big Country*
    c. *Cat on a Hot Tin Roof*
19. a. Gig Young
    b. *They Shoot Horses, Don't They?*
    c. Jane Fonda, Michael Sarrazin, Susannah York, Red Buttons, and Bonnie Bedelia
20. a. Charles Coburn
    b. *The More the Merrier*
    c. Jean Arthur and Joel McCrea
    d. *Kings Row*

Spencer Tracy
1. *Captains Courageous*
2. *Boys Town*
3. *The Show-Off*

4. *20,000 Years in Sing Sing*
5. *Stanley and Livingstone*
6. *Edison the Man*
7. *San Francisco*
8. *Boom Town*
9. *Test Pilot*
10. *Boom Town*
11. *Pat and Mike*
12. *Bad Day at Black Rock*
13. *Father of the Bride* (the sequel: *Father's Little Dividend*)
14. *The Actress*
15. *Inherit the Wind*
16. *The Old Man and the Sea*
17. *Judgment at Nuremberg*
18. *Tortilla Flat*
19. *Thirty Seconds Over Tokyo*
20. *Guess Who's Coming to Dinner*

Best Supporting Actor Quiz Number Two
1. a. Donald Crisp
   b. *How Green Was My Valley*
   c. Roddy McDowall
2. a. Walter Matthau
   b. *The Fortune Cookie*
   c. *The Odd Couple*
3. a. Robert De Niro
   b. *The Godfather Part II*
   c. *Bang the Drum Slowly*
   d. *Taxi Driver*
4. Arthur Kennedy
5. a. James Dunn
   b. *A Tree Grows in Brooklyn*
   c. Dorothy McGuire
6. a. Ben Johnson
   b. *The Last Picture Show*
   c. Timothy Bottoms and Jeff Bridges
7. a. Dean Jagger
   b. *Twelve O'Clock High*

c. *My Son John*
8. a. George Chakiris
   b. *West Side Story*
   c. Natalie Wood
9. a. George Burns
   b. *The Sunshine Boys*
   c. Walter Matthau
10. a. Hugh Griffith
    b. *Ben-Hur*
    c. *Tom Jones*
11. a. Edmond O'Brien
    b. *The Barefoot Contessa*
    c. Ava Gardner
12. a. Jack Albertson
    b. *The Subject Was Roses*
    c. Patricia Neal
13. a. Walter Huston
    b. *The Treasure of the Sierra Madre*
    c. *Dodsworth*
14. a. Martin Balsam
    b. *A Thousand Clowns*
    c. *Psycho*
15. a. Ed Begley
    b. *Sweet Bird of Youth*
    c. *Patterns*
16. a. Red Buttons
    b. *Sayonara*
    c. *The Poseidon Adventure*
17. Charles Bickford
18. a. Karl Malden
    b. *A Streetcar Named Desire*
    c. *Baby Doll*
19. a. Frank Sinatra
    b. *From Here to Eternity*
    c. *The Man With the Golden Arm*
20. a. Gene Kelly
    b. *Anchors Aweigh,
       Take Me Out to the Ball Game,*
       and *On the Town*

Bette Davis

1. *Jezebel*
2. a. *Dark Victory*
   b. Geraldine Fitzgerald
   c. George Brent
3. a. *Juarez*
   b. Brian Aherne
4. a. *Beyond the Forest*
   b. Joseph Cotten
   c. *Who's Afraid of Virginia Woolf?*
5. a. *Mr. Skeffington*
   b. Claude Rains
   c. No one; the character did not appear in the film.
6. a. *Now, Voyager*
   b. Paul Henreid
   c. Gladys Cooper
7. a. *The Letter*
   b. *The Little Foxes*
   c. James Stephenson for *The Letter*; Patricia Collinge and Teresa Wright for *The Little Foxes*
8. a. *All About Eve*
   b. Gary Merrill
   c. Thelma Ritter
9. a. *The Bride Came C.O.D.*
   b. *The Man Who Came to Dinner*
   c. *June Bride*
10. *In This Our Life*
11. *The Old Maid* and *Old Acquaintance*
12. *Whatever Happened to Baby Jane?*
13. *Hush . . . Hush, Sweet Charlotte*
14. *The Catered Affair*
15. a. *The Corn Is Green*
    b. John Dall
    c. Emlyn Williams
16. William Wyler
17. *Watch on the Rhine*
18. *The Private Lives of Elizabeth and Essex* and *The Virgin Queen*
19. a. *Thank Your Lucky Stars*
    b. "They're Either Too Young or Too Old"

20. a. *Dark Victory*
    b. *All About Eve*
    c. *Beyond the Forest*
    d. *The Little Foxes*
    e. *Of Human Bondage*
    f. *Now, Voyager*
    g. *Jezebel*
    h. *The Petrified Forest*
    i. *The Corn Is Green*
    j. *The Letter*

Best Supporting Actress Quiz Number One
1. a. Gale Sondergaard
   b. *Anthony Adverse*
   c. Bob Hope
2. a. Ruth Gordon
   b. *Rosemary's Baby*
   c. Mia Farrow
3. a. Beatrice Straight
   b. *Network*
   c. William Holden
4. Ann Blyth and Eve Arden
5. *Pride of the Yankees* (for Best Actress) and *Mrs. Miniver* (for Best Supporting Actress)
6. Donna Reed for *From Here to Eternity* (1953) and Shirley Jones for *Elmer Gantry* (1960)
7. Thelma Ritter
8. *All About Eve, The Mating Season, With a Song in My Heart, Pickup on South Street, Pillow Talk,* and *Bird Man of Alcatraz*
9. a. Lee Grant
   b. *Detective Story*
   c. *Shampoo*
   d. *The Landlord* and *Voyage of the Damned*
10. Katina Paxinou
11. Ingrid Bergman, Akim Tamiroff, Vladimir Sokoloff, Mikhail Rasumny, Fortunio Bonanova, and Alexander Granach
12. a. Anne Revere
    b. *A Place in the Sun* (Clift), *The Song of Bernadette* (Jones), *Body and Soul* (Garfield), *National Velvet* (Taylor), and *Gentleman's Agreement* (Peck)
    c. *National Velvet*

13. a. Mary Astor
  b. *The Great Lie*
14. *The Maltese Falcon*
15. a. Dorothy Malone
  b. *Written on the Wind*
  c. *The Big Sleep*
  d. *Too Much, Too Soon*
16. a. Gloria Grahame
  b. *The Bad and the Beautiful*
  c. Dick Powell
  d. Lana Turner, Kirk Douglas, Walter Pidgeon, Barry Sullivan, and Gilbert Roland
17. a. *Crossfire*
  b. Robert Young and Robert Mitchum
18. a. Agnes Moorehead
  b. *Mrs. Parkington, Johnny Belinda,* and *Hush...Hush, Sweet Charlotte*
19. a. Patty Duke
  b. *The Miracle Worker*
  c. *Valley of the Dolls*
20. a. Ethel Barrymore
  b. *None But the Lonely Heart*
  c. *The Spiral Staircase*
21. a. Jane Darwell
  b. *The Grapes of Wrath*
22. a. Anne Baxter
  b. *The Razor's Edge*
  c. W. Somerset Maugham
23. a. *The Magnificent Ambersons*
  b. *I Confess*
  c. *All About Eve*
24. a. Tatum O'Neal
  b. *Paper Moon*
  c. Ryan O'Neal
25. a. Hattie McDaniel
  b. *Gone With the Wind*
  c. Mammy

1951

1. a. *A Place in the Sun*
   b. *A Streetcar Named Desire*
2. *An American in Paris*
3. *The African Queen*
4. a. *Detective Story*
   b. Kirk Douglas
   c. Joseph Wiseman and Michael Strong
5. a. Eleanor Parker
   b. *Caged* and *Interrupted Melody*
6. a. *Death of a Salesman*
   b. Fredric March, Mildred Dunnock, and Kevin McCarthy
   c. Willy, Linda, and Biff Loman
7. a. *Strangers on a Train*
   b. Robert Walker (Bruno Anthony) and Farley Granger (Guy Haines)
   c. Ruth Roman
8. a. *Quo Vadis*
   b. Robert Taylor and Deborah Kerr
9. a. *Bright Victory*
   b. Arthur Kennedy
10. a. *The Red Badge of Courage*
    b. Audie Murphy
    c. Bill Mauldin
11. a. *Ace in the Hole*
    b. *The Big Carnival*
    c. Jan Sterling
12. a. *No Highway in the Sky*
    b. James Stewart and Marlene Dietrich
13. a. *Decision Before Dawn*
    b. Oskar Werner
    c. *Fourteen Hours*
    d. Grace Kelly
14. a. *The Great Caruso*
    b. Mario Lanza
    c. Ann Blyth
15. a. *Show Boat*
    b. Kathryn Grayson, Howard Keel, and Ava Gardner
    c. Irene Dunne, Allan Jones, and Helen Morgan

16. a. *Royal Wedding*
    b. Sarah Churchill
17. a. *People Will Talk*
    b. Cary Grant
    c. Jeanne Crain
18. a. *The Mudlark*
    b. Irene Dunne
    c. Alec Guinness
19. a. *Teresa*
    b. Pier Angeli
    c. John Ericson
20. a. *The Blue Veil*
    b. Joan Blondell
    c. *Here Comes the Groom*

Best Supporting Actress Quiz Number Two

1. a. Fay Bainter
   b. *Jezebel*
   c. *White Banners*
2. a. Alice Brady
   b. *In Old Chicago*
   c. *My Man Godfrey*
3. a. Josephine Hull
   b. *Harvey*
   c. *Arsenic and Old Lace*
4. a. Jo Van Fleet
   b. *East of Eden*
   c. Raymond Massey
5. a. Eva Marie Saint
   b. *On the Waterfront*
   c. *North by Northwest*
6. a. Eileen Heckart
   b. *Butterflies Are Free*
   c. Edward Albert
7. a. Celeste Holm
   b. *Gentleman's Agreement*
   c. *All About Eve*
8. a. Ingrid Bergman
   b. *Murder on the Orient Express*
   c. Albert Finney
9. a. Kim Hunter
   b. *A Streetcar Named Desire*
   c. *Planet of the Apes*
10. a. Cloris Leachman
    b. *The Last Picture Show*
    c. *Young Frankenstein*
11. a. Mercedes McCambridge
    b. *All the King's Men*
    c. *Giant*
12. a. Miyoshi Umeki
    b. *Sayonara*
    c. *Flower Drum Song*
13. a. Margaret Rutherford
    b. *The V.I.P.'s*
    c. *The Importance of Being Earnest*

14. a. Wendy Hiller
   b. *Separate Tables*
   c. *Pygmalion* and *Major Barbara*
15. a. Rita Moreno
   b. *West Side Story*
   c. *The King and I*
16. a. Sandy Dennis
   b. *Who's Afraid of Virginia Woolf?*
   c. *Up the Down Staircase*
17. a. Lila Kedrova
   b. *Zorba the Greek*
18. a. Estelle Parsons
   b. *Bonnie and Clyde*
   c. *Rachel, Rachel*
19. a. Goldie Hawn
   b. *Cactus Flower*
   c. *Shampoo*
20. a. Ethel Barrymore and Ethel Waters
   b. Ellen Burstyn and Cloris Leachman
   c. Celeste Holm and Thelma Ritter
   d. Olivia de Havilland and Hattie McDaniel
   e. Celeste Holm and Elsa Lanchester
   f. Diane Cilento, Edith Evans, and Joyce Redman

What's in a Name?

Quiz Number One	*Quiz Number Two*
1. k	**1.** k
2. f	**2.** f
3. i	**3.** j
4. l	**4.** c
5. j	**5.** l
6. b	**6.** i
7. h	**7.** h
8. a	**8.** a
9. g	**9.** b
10. d	**10.** d
11. c	**11.** g
12. e	**12.** e

Two-Timers
1. a. Vivien Leigh
   b. *Gone With the Wind* and *A Streetcar Named Desire*
   c. Scarlett O'Hara and Blanche DuBois
2. a. *Waterloo Bridge*
   b. *A Yank at Oxford*
3. a. Fredric March
   b. *Dr. Jekyll and Mr. Hyde* and *The Best Years of Our Lives*
4. a. *The Barretts of Wimpole Street*
   b. *A Star Is Born*
   c. *Death of a Salesman*
   d. *Nothing Sacred*
   e. *The Adventures of Mark Twain*
   f. *Inherit the Wind*
5. a. Helen Hayes
   b. *The Sin of Madelon Claudet* and *Airport*
   c. *A Farewell to Arms*
6. a. Glenda Jackson
   b. *Women in Love* and *A Touch of Class*
   c. Alan Bates or Oliver Reed (in *Women*) and George Segal (in *Touch*)
7. a. Shelley Winters
   b. *The Diary of Anne Frank* and *A Patch of Blue*
8. a. Elizabeth Taylor
   b. *Butterfield 8* and *Who's Afraid of Virginia Woolf?*
   c. Eddie Fisher (*Butterfield*) and Richard Burton (*Virginia Woolf*)
9. a. *A Place in the Sun, Raintree County*, and *Suddenly, Last Summer*
   b. Shelley Winters (*Place*), Eva Marie Saint (*Raintree*), and Katharine Hepburn (*Suddenly*)
10. a. Peter Ustinov
    b. *Spartacus* and *Topkapi*
    c. *Quo Vadis*
11. a. Marlon Brando
    b. *On the Waterfront* and *The Godfather*
    c. Rod Steiger
    d. Al Pacino and James Caan
12. a. *The Wild One*

b. *The Men*
c. *A Streetcar Named Desire*
d. *The Young Lions*
e. *Viva Zapata!*
f. *Sayonara*
g. *Julius Caesar*
h. *Guys and Dolls*
i. *Desirée*

13. a. Olivia de Havilland
b. *To Each His Own*
c. John Lund

14. a. *The Heiress*
b. *The Snake Pit*

15. She appeared with Errol Flynn in *Captain Blood, The Charge of the Light Brigade, The Adventures of Robin Hood, Four's a Crowd, Dodge City, The Private Lives of Elizabeth and Essex, Santa Fe Trail*, and *They Died With Their Boots On*, and they both made guest appearances in *Thank Your Lucky Stars*.

16. a. Ingrid Bergman
b. *Gaslight* and *Anastasia*
c. Charles Boyer

17. a. *Casablanca*
b. *Notorious* or *Indiscreet*
c. *Spellbound*

18. a. Gary Cooper
b. *Sergeant York* and *High Noon*
c. *For Whom the Bell Tolls* or *Saratoga Trunk*

19. a. Anthony Quinn
b. *Viva Zapata!* and *Lust for Life*
c. Marlon Brando (Zapata) and Kirk Douglas (van Gogh)

20. Luise Rainer

21. Jack Lemmon

22. a. *Save the Tiger*
b. Jack Gilford

23. a. *Mister Roberts*
b. Henry Fonda
c. James Cagney

24. a. *The Days of Wine and Roses*
b. *Some Like It Hot*

c. *The Apartment*
25. a. Bette Davis in *A Stolen Life* and *Dead Ringer*
    b. Olivia de Havilland in *The Dark Mirror*

General Quiz Number Two
1. a. Charles Chaplin for *The Great Dictator*, Sylvester Stallone for *Rocky*, and Orson Welles for *Citizen Kane*
    b. Welles (and Herman J. Mankiewicz) won the Oscar for Best Original Screenplay.
2. *The Way We Were* (for Best Musical Score and Best Song) and *The Sting* (for Best Musical Adaptation)
3. a. *East of Eden, Rebel Without a Cause*, and *Giant*
    b. *East of Eden* and *Giant*
4. They are all parents of Oscar winners. Michael Douglas won as producer of *One Flew Over the Cuckoo's Nest*, John Huston won for his screenplay and direction of *The Treasure of the Sierra Madre*, and Jane Fonda, Liza Minnelli, and Tatum O'Neal won as performers.
5. a. *Stella Dallas*
    b. *Double Indemnity*
    c. *Ball of Fire*
    d. *Sorry, Wrong Number*
6. All have won Oscars in films directed by William Wyler.
7. a. *Mutiny on the Bounty*
    b. Clark Gable, Charles Laughton, and Franchot Tone
    c. Victor McLaglen
8. a. Vivien Leigh, Marlon Brando, Kim Hunter, and Karl Malden
    b. Jane Wyman, Lew Ayres, Agnes Moorehead, and Charles Bickford
    c. Carole Lombard, William Powell, Alice Brady, and Mischa Auer
    d. Gloria Swanson, William Holden, Nancy Olson, and Erich von Stroheim
    e. Faye Dunaway; Peter Finch and William Holden; Beatrice Straight; Ned Beatty
    f. Faye Dunaway; Warren Beatty; Estelle Parsons; Gene Hackman and Michael J. Pollard

g. Deborah Kerr; Montgomery Clift and Burt Lancaster; Donna Reed; Frank Sinatra

h. Elizabeth Taylor, Richard Burton, Sandy Dennis, and George Segal

i. Greer Garson; Walter Pidgeon; Dame May Whitty and Teresa Wright; Henry Travers

j. Ingrid Bergman, Gary Cooper, Katina Paxinou, and Akim Tamiroff

k. Katharine Hepburn, Spencer Tracy, Beah Richards, and Cecil Kellaway

9. a. Anne Baxter and Bette Davis; Celeste Holm and Thelma Ritter; George Sanders

b. Marlon Brando; Eva Marie Saint; Lee J. Cobb, Karl Malden, and Rod Steiger

c. Albert Finney; Diane Cilento, Edith Evans, and Joyce Redman; Hugh Griffith

d. Al Pacino; Talia Shire; Robert De Niro, Michael V. Gazzo, and Lee Strasberg

10. a. Ida Lupino

b. *The Hard Way*

11. a. *From Here to Eternity*

b. *The Search*

c. *Judgment at Nuremberg*

d. *A Place in the Sun*

12. a. Olivia de Havilland and Joan Fontaine in 1941; Lynn and Vanessa Redgrave in 1966

b. *Hold Back the Dawn* (de Havilland), *Suspicion* (Fontaine), *Morgan!* (Vanessa Redgrave), and *Georgy Girl* (Lynn Redgrave)

13. a. *The Godfather, Serpico, The Godfather Part II*, and *Dog Day Afternoon*

b. Francis Ford Coppola (the *Godfather* films) and Sidney Lumet (*Serpico* and *Dog Day Afternoon*)

14. All won for playing alcoholics. Heflin, not covered elsewhere in this book, won his award for *Johnny Eager*.

15. a. Deborah Kerr

b. *Edward, My Son; From Here to Eternity; The King and I; Heaven Knows, Mr. Allison; Separate Tables; The Sundowners*

16. All have won Oscars in films directed by William Wyler.
17. a. James Dean, Peter Finch, and Spencer Tracy
    b. Peter Finch won for *Network*. Tracy, of course, won two awards during his lifetime.
18. *Penny Serenade* and *None But the Lonely Heart*
19. Fonda's only nomination was for playing Tom Joad in *The Grapes of Wrath*.
20. a. *My Sister Eileen*
    b. *Mourning Becomes Electra*
    c. *Sister Kenny*
    d. *Auntie Mame*
21. a. *His Girl Friday*
    b. *The Front Page*
    c. Cary Grant
    d. Howard Hawks
22. a. John Garfield
    b. *Body and Soul*
    c. *Gentleman's Agreement*
    d. *Four Daughters*
23. a. Gene Kelly (*An American in Paris*)
    b. Jerome Robbins (*West Side Story*)
    c. Onna White (*Oliver!*)
24. Jack Albertson, Ernest Borgnine, Red Buttons, Gene Hackman, and Shelley Winters
25. a. 10   f. 6
    b. 2 and 9   g. 5
    c. 4   h. 1
    d. 8   i. 11 and 12
    e. 3   j. 7

True or False
  1. True
  2. False   (Dame Judith's only nomination was for *Rebecca*)
  3. False   (Perkins made his debut in 1953 in *The Actress*)
  4. True   (She was heard as Addie Ross in *A Letter to Three Wives*)
  5. True   (*Smash-Up—The Story of a Woman*, *My Foolish Heart*, and *I'll Cry Tomorrow*)

6. False
7. True   (He played Judge Hardy in *A Family Affair*, and Lewis Stone played the role in all subsequent films)
8. False   (She was nominated for *The More the Merrier*)
9. True
10. False   (Russell's first nomination came later, for *My Sister Eileen*)
11. False   (Kelly's only nomination was for *Anchors Aweigh*)
12. True   (Davis in *Whatever Happened to Baby Jane?* and Hepburn in *Summertime*)
13. False   (Taylor was not nominated for *A Place in the Sun*)
14. True   (*The Iron Petticoat*)
15. False   (Bogart appeared in *The Oklahoma Kid* and *Virginia City*)
16. True
17. False   (Blondell's only nomination was for *The Blue Veil*)
18. False   (Laurence Olivier is tied with Tracy at nine nominations)
19. False   (Marlon Brando refused his award for *The Godfather*)
20. True

LIST OF PICTURES

(with explanation and/or names
of those in each picture)
AND PAGE NUMBERS

Page
2   Frank Borzage and Janet Gaynor
10   The first awards banquet at the Hollywood Roosevelt Hotel
12   Emil Jannings
15   Hans Kraly, William De Mille, Mary Pickford, and Warner Baxter
16   Louis B. Mayer, Helen Hayes, and Lionel Barrymore
18   Clark Gable
      inset: Norma Shearer
21   Shirley Temple and Claudette Colbert
24   Louis B. Mayer, Victor McLaglen, and Clark Gable
25   *top*: Jerome Robbins and Gene Kelly
      bottom left: John Wayne and Barbra Streisand
      bottom right: Leslie Caron and Mike Nichols
26   Charles Chaplin with others onstage at the Dorothy Chandler Pavilion, after he received an honorary Academy Award
      inset: Roger Moore and Liv Ullmann with Sacheen Littlefeather, who read a message from the absent Marlon Brando
28   Frank Capra, D. W. Griffith, Jean Hersholt, Henry B. Walthall, Frank Lloyd, Cecil B. De Mille, and Donald Crisp
31   1936 awards before being presented at the Biltmore Hotel banquet
33   Spencer Tracy, Bette Davis
35   Bette Davis and Victor McLaglen

37   *left*: Walter Brennan and Gale Sondergaard
     right: Thomas Mitchell
38   Judy Garland and Mickey Rooney
39   Spencer Tracy and Vivien Leigh
42   Hattie McDaniel and Fay Bainter
43   *top left*: Raquel Welch and Liza Minnelli
     top right: Jane Fonda
     bottom: Jack Lemmon and Groucho Marx, accepting an honorary Academy Award
44   *top*: Charles Bronson, Jill Ireland, and Tatum O'Neal
     bottom left: John Houseman, Ernest Borgnine, and Cybill Shepherd
     bottom right: Katharine Hepburn, in the only appearance she has ever made at the Academy Awards ceremonies, presenting the Irving Thalberg Award to Laurence Weingarten
48   Alfred Lunt, Lynn Fontanne, Jane Darwell, and Walter Brennan
51   Gary Cooper, Joan Fontaine, Wendell Willkie, Mary Astor, and Donald Crisp
53   Joan Fontaine and Olivia de Havilland with Burgess Meredith
55   Van Heflin, Greer Garson, James Cagney, and Theresa Wright
59   *top left*: Francis Ford Coppola with father, Carmine Coppola, sister Talia Shire, and wife at the Board of Governors Ball following the 1974 ceremonies
     top right: Art Carney and Glenda Jackson
     bottom: Ingrid Bergman
60   *top left*: George Burns
     top right: Jill Ireland and Louise Fletcher
     bottom: Michael Douglas, Milos Forman, Louise Fletcher, Jack Nicholson, and Saul Zaentz
61   Paul Lukas, Jennifer Jones, Katina Paxinou, and Charles Coburn
64   *left*: Joan Crawford
     right: Irving Thalberg Award winner Darryl F. Zanuck with Thalberg's widow, Norma Shearer, and Bob Hope
65   Peggy Ann Garner, James Dunn, Anne Revere, and Ray Milland
66   Ray Milland delivering a special award for *Henry V* to Laurence Olivier on the set of *Hamlet*
69   1948 Master of Ceremonies Robert Montgomery onstage at the Academy Theatre

74   *top*: Edmund Gwenn, Claire Trevor, Walter Huston, and Celeste Holm
bottom: Humphrey Bogart, Danny Kaye, Arthur Freed, and George Stevens

81   John Wayne accepting for Gary Cooper. Janet Gaynor presents the award onstage, with Bob Hope, at the Pantages Theatre.

84   Walter Brennan, Donna Reed, Frank Sinatra, and Mercedes McCambridge

89   Marlon Brando and Bette Davis

94   Grace Kelly and William Holden

97   Jerry Lewis onstage at the Pantages Theatre

98   Edmund O'Brien, Jo Van Fleet, Jack Lemmon, and Eva Marie Saint

99   Mike Todd with his wife, Elizabeth Taylor

102   Simone Signoret

103   Joanne Woodward, Red Buttons, Miyoshi Umeki, and Jean Simmons (accepting for Alec Guinness)

104   Burl Ives, Susan Hayward, David Niven, and Ingrid Bergman

106   Edmond O'Brien and Shelley Winters

108   Outside the RKO Pantages Theatre on Hollywood Boulevard (1959)

111   Inside the Santa Monica Auditorium. Best Actress Elizabeth Taylor is escorted to the stage by her husband, Eddie Fisher.

112   Peter Ustinov, Shirley Jones, Burt Lancaster, Elizabeth Taylor, and Billy Wilder

114   Gregory Peck, Patty Duke, Joan Crawford (accepting for Anne Bancroft), and Ed Begley

117   Gregory Peck, Annabella (accepting for Patricia Neal), Sidney Poitier, and Anne Bancroft

119   Rex Harrison and Audrey Hepburn

121   *top left*: Beatrice Straight
top right: Barbra Streisand singing the winning song for 1976
bottom: Muhammad Ali and Sylvester Stallone

122   *top*: Academy Award winners at the Academy's new building on Wilshire Boulevard in Beverly Hills
bottom left: Jason Robards and Tatum O'Neal
bottom right: Louise Fletcher and Faye Dunaway

123   Outside the Santa Monica Auditorium preceding the 1967 ceremonies

160   A standing ovation in the Dorothy Chandler Pavilion